BAKING for GIFT-GIVING

ALSO BY LISA YOCKELSON

The Efficient Epicure

Glorious Gifts from Your Kitchen

Country Pies

Country Cakes

Country Cookies

Fruit Desserts

Brownies and Blondies

American Baking Classics

BAKING
for
GIFT-GIVING

• • •

LISA YOCKELSON

HarperCollins*Publishers*

to the memory of

my parents

HarperCollins books may be purchased for educational, business, or sales promotional use. For information please write: Special Markets Department, HarperCollins Publishers, Inc., 10 East 53rd Street, New York, NY 10022.

FIRST EDITION

Designed by Helene Berinsky

Library of Congress Cataloging-in-Publication Data
Yockelson, Lisa.
Baking for gift-giving / Lisa Yockelson. — lst ed.
p.   cm. — (American baking classics)
Includes index.
ISBN 0-06-016750-5 (cloth)
1. Baking.   2. Gifts.   I. Title.   II. Series.
TX763.Y63   1993
641.7'1—dc20   93-16899

95 96 97 DT/RRD 10 9 8 7 6 5 4 3

ACKNOWLEDGMENTS

This volume, *Baking for Gift-Giving*, was inspired by years of baking food gifts. Do I go anywhere without a pound cake in hand, a few dozen cookies, a plump loaf of bread or a tin of muffins? Hardly. Something fresh from the oven is always eagerly received by friends, who quickly ask for the recipe. For their constant blessings and lively appetites, my gratitude to everyone who, over and over again, ate their way through much of what you see recorded in this cookbook.

In numerous and diverse ways, I am fortunate to have ongoing support for this series from Susan Friedland, my editor at HarperCollins, and Susan Lescher, my literary agent. Both, the voice of reason and fine taste, understand my delightful obsession with the baking process. And, all kinds of thanks to: Joseph Montebello, Creative Director at HarperCollins; Carolyn Larson, assistant to Susan Lescher at Lescher and Lescher, Limited; Ann Amernick, cookbook author and pastry chef; Barbara Witt, consultant and cookbook author; Carol Mason, consultant and corporate chef; Penelope Pate-Greene, specialty food consultant; and Pat Brown, editor and consultant, for their endless good cheer.

Contents

· 1 ·

Giving Home-Baked Food Gifts

Food gifts, particularly baked goods, are irresistible—who would turn down a bag full of just-made chocolate chip cookies, a buttery loaf cake loaded with chopped fruit and nuts or a basket heaped with muffins? It seems that something home-baked, fresh from the oven and enticingly packaged, is appreciated more than anything else.

Whatever we bake at home has a natural, handcrafted and, occasionally, rustic appearance. This, and the high-quality ingredients used, is what distinguishes handmade baked goods and makes them all the more appealing. To my eye, the casual, homey look is what good baking is all about—consider craggy oatmeal cookies, giant muffins thickset with berries, a tea bread with the characteristic crackled top.

Cookies, loaf cakes, keeping cakes, loaf breads and rolls, muffins and biscuits are all ideal to bring as a gift if you are a weekend guest, as your contribution to a bring-a-dish supper, tea or coffee hour, school or charity bake sale.

When choosing a recipe, take into consideration the event for which you are baking. For pot-luck suppers or large family gatherings, big cakes or dozens of sturdy drop cookies would be a good selection. The cookies, once wrapped, can be piled into tins or baskets. Muffins, small cookies, biscuits, rolls and loaf cakes make fine gifts for bringing to a weekend or summer house, for you can be sure that they will be enjoyed over the following days. Large cookies, tea cakes, bite-size muffins or biscuits also make handy bread-and-butter hostess gifts, packaged in glossy white, silver or gold paper bags.

WRAPPING AND PACKAGING BAKED GOODS

The cookies, cakes and small breads in this book are designed to pack up in standard containers, such as bakery boxes and cookie tins. Search hardware and variety stores for good-looking tins, bolts of fabric and lace, ribbons, raffia and other packaging material and decorations. Keep a selection of shiny white or gold paper doilies in all sizes and shapes (rounds, hearts, ovals and rectangles), coated paper boxes and very thin florist's wire on hand to make assembling each gift easy. The holiday season (or just after) is an excellent time to stock up on plain white and solid gold-colored tins, boxes and wrappings.

Clear plastic food storage bags, available in a variety of sizes, are handy for enclosing cookies, tea breads and loaves, muffins, biscuits and the like. Good-quality plastic wrap or clear cellophane (both food-safe), available in rolls, can be used for wrapping large cakes, individual loaves or cookies. *One very important note: All wrapping material that comes in contact with food, including bags, plastic wrap and cellophane, should be designated as food-safe, and all food should be wrapped or bagged **first** before assembling in baskets, tins or any other type of container.*

Other packaging thoughts

FOR COOKIES: The time-honored cookie tin (with a tight-fitting lid), lined with a doily, is the classic container. First wrap the cookies in food-safe plastic or cellophane and assemble them neatly in the tin. Wrap cookies, two or three to a bundle, and layer in a basket. Pile the cookies onto a very large sheet of clear cellophane, bring the four corners together and tie with cord or ribbon; place in a flat basket or galvanized tin pail lined with large doilies or a length of fabric. Tuck small, wrapped cookies into new, clean white cartons generally used for Oriental food carry-out (these can be purchased in bulk from a paper goods store).

FOR LOAF BREADS, TEA CAKES AND LOAF CAKES: Slide your bread or cake into clear food storage bags and tie up the open end with a length of cord or ribbon. Enclose the bread or cake in a sheet of plastic wrap or clear cellophane, tuck in the ends as if you were wrapping a package and seal; then place the loaf in a miniature, colorful shopping bag. Small bags can be filled first with a cushion of curly moss before adding the carefully wrapped loaf or cake; let a few fluffs of moss show at the top of the bag. Or, for a special gift, place a *wrapped* loaf of bread (or tea cake) on an antique bread board or bread plate and enclose both in a large sheet of clear cellophane, bringing up the cellophane into a tight topknot; tie with cord.

FOR LARGE "KEEPING" CAKES: A plain white bakery box, with a cardboard cake circle placed on the bottom (both available at a paper goods store, or some kitchen equipment stores) is a simple and effective container for big cakes baked in tube pans. Wrap the cake. Place a paper doily on the cake circle before you set on the cake. Tie a pretty satin ribbon around the box and garnish with an ornament, if you wish.

FOR MUFFINS AND BISCUITS: Pile the wrapped muffins or biscuits in a clear bag or heavy paper gift bag, and tie up the bag with ribbon, cord or raffia. Plain brown paper bags (available in bulk quantities), new and clean, can be used to hold a batch of wrapped biscuits or muffins; the traditional brown sack looks best finished off with gold, beige and brown ribbons. A jar of jam or a small wooden spreader is a thoughtful addition to a gift of muffins or biscuits.

· 2 ·

Ingredients and Baking Supplies

When baking, take your cue from professional kitchens: Have all ingredients measured and the appropriate piece of equipment prepared (most times, lightly buttered and floured, or lined with lengths of kitchen parchment paper) before you begin to bake.

It's handy to incorporate the concept of the "ready tray" in your baking kitchen: Just portion out and arrange the ingredients in the order they are to be used. In this way, it's nearly impossible to forget that crucial teaspoon of baking powder or baking soda in the batter, the melted butter or stray teaspoon of vanilla extract.

Look over the recipe, assembling the ingredients from the pantry as you do so, then measure them out. If the recipe indicates that the flour is to be whisked or sifted with leavening, spices and the like, combine the mixture and add that to the lineup of ingredients. Set out the dairy ingredients, such as eggs and milk, ahead of time to take off the chill and, in the case of butter, to soften it into a malleable condition; this step is particularly important if you are to have your creamed cake, cookie and muffin batters achieve a silky goodness and therefore bake up light and tender. Also, working in this organized fashion insures that the flow of baking will be smooth and stream-lined—even if the telephone or doorbell rings.

The following list of ingredients is a brief overview of the pantry staples (flour, sugar, leavenings, extracts and chocolate), dairy products, dried fruit and nuts used in the recipes that follow. Keep the basics in your pantry; they are easy to store and are fundamental to a respectable baking kitchen. Some of the recipes can be made from simple and essential ingredients alone, which, if stocked, make spur-of-the-moment baking a breeze.

FLOUR: Bleached all-purpose flour; bleached cake flour; whole wheat flour; bread flour

GRAINS: "Old-fashioned" rolled oats; "quick-cooking" (not instant) rolled oats

SWEETENERS: Plain granulated sugar; superfine sugar, also know as "bar" or "dessert" sugar, available in 1-pound boxes; light brown sugar and dark brown sugar, available in 1-pound boxes (firmly press the sugar into cups used for measuring dry ingredients); confectioners' sugar, also known as pow-dered sugar, available in 1-pound boxes; light molasses; honey; pure maple syrup

BUTTER, MARGARINE, SHORTENING AND OIL: Fresh, not previously frozen, unsalted butter; good-quality stick (not whipped) margarine; plain solid shortening (Crisco); plain vegetable oil (such as soybean or canola)

MILK, CREAM AND CREAM CHEESE: Whole milk; half-and-half; buttermilk; evaporated milk; heavy cream; light cream; sour cream; cream cheese (avail-able in 3-ounce and 8-ounce packages)

EGGS: All of the recipes in this book use extra-large eggs.

LEAVENINGS: Baking powder; baking soda; active dry yeast (available in 1/4-ounce packets or 4-ounce jars)

EXTRACTS AND FLAVORINGS: Vanilla extract; lemon extract; almond extract; whole vanilla beans. Use pure extracts for the best flavor.

SPICES: Ground allspice; ground cinnamon; ground cloves; ground ginger; ground cardamom; whole nutmegs for grating; salt

CHOCOLATE AND CANDY BARS: Unsweetened chocolate (available in 8-ounce boxes, each square weighing 1 ounce); unsweetened cocoa powder; semisweet chocolate chips (available in 12-ounce bags); semisweet mint-flavored chocolate chips (available in 10-ounce bags); miniature semisweet chocolate chips (available in 12-ounce bags); milk chocolate candy bars (available in 1.55-ounce, 3-ounce, 4-ounce and 7-ounce bars); bittersweet chocolate candy bars (available in 3-ounce bars); chocolate-covered almond toffee candy (available in 1.4-ounce bars)

NUTS, SEEDS AND DRIED FRUIT: English walnuts; Brazil nuts; pecans; unsalted macadamia nuts; almonds; sunflower seeds; dark raisins; moist dried currants; pitted dates; moist pitted prunes

In baked goods, the flavor of walnuts, pecans, Brazil nuts and macadamia nuts is much improved by a preliminary toasting before incorporating them into a batter. Spread out the nuts on a baking sheet and toast in a preheated 350-degree oven for about 5 to 7 minutes. Cool completely before using. If nuts are to be sprinkled on top of a batter before baking, it is unnecessary to toast them.

EQUIPMENT

The cakes, cookies and breads in this book are baked in standard loaf pans (10 by 5 by 3 inches; 9 by 5 by 3 inches; 8 by 4 by 3 inches; and 7 by 4 by 3 inches); miniature loaf pans (5 by 3 by 2 3/4 inches); a fluted tube pan (9 inches in diameter by 4 1/2 inches deep); a plain tube pan (10 inches in diameter by a scant 5 inches deep); regular muffin tins (2 3/4 inches in diameter by 1 3/8 inches deep); jumbo muffin tins (a scant 4 inches in diameter by 1 3/4 inches deep); square baking pans (8 by 8 by 2 inches and 9 by 9 by 2 inches); 13-by-9-by-2-inch baking pans; and cookie sheets (14 inches by 18 inches) made of good-quality aluminum.

The rusks on page 30 and page 33 use a slightly unusual piece of equipment—shallow metal ice cube trays with the dividers removed. With this type of pan the batter bakes into a rectangular "cake" that can be cut into slices with ease. The pan eliminates the tedious procedure of forming the dough into logs and chilling it until it is easy to handle; adding additional flour to make a stiffer dough that is easier to manage (and, for me, way too floury-tasting) is unnecessary. Old-fashioned metal ice cube trays are still available at hardware stores; if you have a choice, buy those that have smooth, rather than pebbly, surfaces. Alternately, the rusk batter can be baked in two 7-by-4-by-3-inch loaf pans. If you are using the loaf pans, increase the baking time about 5 minutes; let the "cakes" cool for 5 to 7 minutes in the pans, invert them carefully onto a cooling rack, then invert again to cool rightside-up.

For plain and fluted tube pans, I prefer to use those lined with a release surface, such as Silverstone® or Teflon®.

In my experience, the most efficient mixer for blending together cake batters and cookie doughs is one where both the bowl and the beaters rotate, allowing you to get a spatula into the bowl and push along the contents easily; mine is a Sunbeam mixer and since I bake so much, I have a collection of them. This mixer is very effective for creaming butter, sugar and eggs together, and lets you incorporate both small and large quantities of flour with ease.

For whipping eggs and granulated sugar together for sponge cake batters, or for kneading yeast doughs by machine, I use a Kitchen Aid. Its beaters spin round and round, and the deep, capacious bowl remains stationary.

Usually, when baking with yeast, I put together a dough in the traditional way—in a large mixing bowl, with a sturdy wooden spoon. I knead the dough by hand, the premier way for judging the texture, "pull" and suppleness. Alternately, a heavy-duty, free-standing mixer equipped with the dough hook—such as the Kitchen Aid mentioned above—is a fine, easy alternative.

Before I bake, I lightly butter and flour the inside of every pan (except a cookie sheet), even if it is treated with a release surface coating. Your hands are the best piece of equipment for this: Spread a film of softened, unsalted butter (using salted butter encourages cakes and breads to stick to the inside of the pan) over the entire interior surface area of the baking pan; this nugget of butter is always in addition to the amount called for in the recipe. If it is a tube pan, plain or fancy, be meticulous about coating the entire tube and deep swirls, especially where the tube meets the base of the pan. Sprinkle a little flour over the inside, then tap it around to form a haze over the butter. Shake out the excess flour over the kitchen sink.

Using a baking spray that contains both vegetable oil and flour is a fast and easy way to prepare a baking pan. It is particularly effective when you are using a fluted tube pan, for the spray can get into all the nooks with ease. A baking spray makes quick work of preparing round or square cake pans, too.

When baking cookies, it is easiest to line the cookie sheets with lengths of kitchen parchment paper designed for use in baking. The paper comes in a 20-square-foot roll, with the same kind of finely serrated cutting edge found on a box of wax paper or aluminum foil. Tear off lengths of paper to fit the size of your pans. Cookies baked on parchment are effortless to slip off with a spatula and the paper can be wiped clean with a damp sponge and used over again on the next baking day.

· 3 ·

Cookies

Cookies are among my favorite bakery sweets to give as gifts, for they are easy to make in quantity and can be layered in all kinds of containers. A batch of drop cookies can be wrapped and piled in brightly colored bags, some of which have clear cellophane windows cut out of one side in a pattern of stars or such seasonal shapes as the Easter bunny or a Christmas tree. The bags are available at cookware and paper goods stores in a variety of bright colors.

Around Thanksgiving, hardware and cookware stores sell cookie tins of all colors and sizes—I usually buy plain white or gold tins, as either color can be customized with seasonal decorations. Line the tins with a paper doily or simulated "leaves" made out of greaseproof paper. Paper leaves come in many sizes and are generally used for lining cheese trays, but I find them useful for arranging on the bottom of a tin before adding the wrapped cookies. While a large tin certainly can hold a whole batch of cookies, it's a good idea to place fragile, shortbreadlike cookies (such as the *Pecan Crescents* on page 14 or *Nutmeg Sugar Tops* on page 22) in several small tins.

A basket of cookies always makes a festive and enticing gift. When choosing a basket for a batch of homemade sweets, remember that you want the overall look to be one of abundance; this is accomplished by picking a relatively small basket and mounding the cookies in it. Line the basket with a large sheet of heavy food-safe cellophane, pile in the cookies, gather up the sides and tie with a length of raffia, ribbon or colored cord. Or wrap the cookies individually or in back-to-back packages of two, then arrange them in the basket.

A SPECIAL BAKING NOTE

Cookies should be baked on thoroughly cooled cookie sheets lined with parchment paper designed to be used in baking. I generally use two cookie sheets, place the mounds or rolled-out shapes of dough on several sheets of parchment, and slide the paper onto the cookie sheet.

I obtain the best results from baking one sheet of cookies at a time on the middle-level rack of the oven. In this way, while one sheet is in the oven, the other is ready to be baked. Avoid baking cookies on sheets that are oven-hot, for the dough would spread and begin to melt down too fast. But, if you want to bake two sheets of cookies at one time, use the upper- and lower-third-level racks and, halfway through the baking time, switch the sheets from top to bottom and front to back to insure even baking.

MORE IDEAS

The following bar cookies, chosen from the first book in my American Baking Classics series, *Brownies and Blondies* (New York: HarperCollins*Publishers*, 1992), make excellent gifts, too: *Classic Chewy Brownies* (pages 18–19); *Chocolate, Walnut and Caramel Brownies* (pages 20–21); *Deep Dish Fudge Brownies* (pages 22–23); *Double Chocolate Walnut Chunk Brownies* (page 26); *Triple Nut Brownies* (page 27); *Rocky Road Brownies* (pages 30–31); *Coffee Chunk Brownies* (page 34); *Classic Blondies* (page 65); *Classic Peanut Butter Blondies* (pages 66–67); *Coconut Blondies* (pages 68–69); *Chocolate Chip Butterscotch Blondies* (pages 70–71); *Date and Walnut Blondies* (page 75); and *Toffee Blondies* (page 80).

Pecan Crescents

◆ *about 5 dozen 2 1/2-inch cookies* ◆

*T*hese shortbreadlike cookies, flecked inside and out with chopped pecans, make a good holiday gift packed in an attractive tin. This is a very old recipe of mine, one which I have tinkered with many times to refine its taste and texture. It produces a dough that is a pleasure to handle.

Pecan Crescents are a superb companion to coffee or tea, a compote of summer berries, goblets of sherbet or ice cream.

*3 cups plus 3 tablespoons unsifted
    all-purpose flour
3 tablespoons plus 1 teaspoon
    cornstarch
1/2 teaspoon baking powder
1/2 teaspoon baking soda
1/4 teaspoon cream of tartar*

*1/4 teaspoon salt
1/4 teaspoon freshly grated nutmeg
3/4 pound (3 sticks) unsalted
    butter, melted and cooled
2/3 cup confectioners' sugar
1 1/4 teaspoons vanilla extract
1 1/2 cups finely chopped pecans*

TO FINISH THE COOKIES:

*About 2 cups confectioners' sugar,
    for dredging the baked cookies*

Preheat the oven to 350 degrees. Line two cookie sheets with lengths of parchment paper.

Sift together the flour, cornstarch, baking powder, baking soda, cream of tartar, salt and nutmeg.

Stir together the butter, 2/3 cup confectioners' sugar and vanilla extract. Stir in half of the sifted mixture, 1 cup pecans, then the remaining sifted mixture.

To form each cookie, take up a heaping teaspoon of dough, roll into a log, form into a crescent and place on the lined cookie sheet, spacing the cookies about 1 1/2 inches apart. Press pinches of the remaining pecans on top of the crescents.

Bake the cookies for about 13 to 15 minutes, or until set. The undersides should be a very pale golden color. After 1 minute, transfer the cookies to cooling racks using a wide metal spatula. Cool for 5 minutes. While the cookies are still warm, carefully dredge them in the confectioners' sugar. Cool completely.

Store in an airtight container.

NOTE: *Lemon Butter Balls*, a variation of this cookie, appeared in the last volume of my country baking series, *Country Cookies: An Old-Fashioned Collection* (New York: Harper & Row, 1990). For the lemon balls, the butter is softened and creamed, rather than melted, and the tang of lemon replaces the vanilla extract and chopped pecans.

Old-Time Chocolate Chip Crisps

◆ *about 5 dozen 3 3/4-inch cookies* ◆

*Y*ears ago, inspired by the time-honored formula for Toll House® cookies, I began baking these crunchy, buttery cookies. Ever since then, the crisps have become a much sought after hostess gift. Over the Christmas holidays, I bundle about 8 cookies in clear cellophane, tie them on either end with ribbon, and give them to friends who drop by.

The formula below, which is one of the oldest cookie recipes in my file, uses more chips and vanilla, and less flour than the traditional Toll House® recipe. Also, I use a combination of unsifted all-purpose flour and cake flour to tenderize the dough and make it brittle-crisp. To make soft and chewy chocolate chip cookies, use the recipe for the *Soft Milk Chocolate Cookies* on page 20 and substitute 2 cups chocolate chips for the chopped milk chocolate candy *or* 4 3-ounce bars of bittersweet chocolate, such as Lindt "Excellence" or Tobler "Tradition." Cut the candy bars into chunks.

These cookies spread while baking, so you should bake 9 mounds of dough on a standard-size sheet at one time.

1 2/3 cups unsifted all-purpose flour
1/3 cup plus 1/2 teaspoon unsifted cake flour
1 teaspoon baking soda
3/4 teaspoon salt
1/2 pound (2 sticks) unsalted butter, softened

1 cup light brown sugar
2/3 cup less 1 tablespoon granulated sugar
2 extra-large eggs
2 1/2 teaspoons vanilla extract
16 ounces (2 1/2 cups, or 1 12-ounce bag plus 1/2 cup) semisweet chocolate chips

Preheat the oven to 375 degrees. Line two cookie sheets with lengths of parchment paper.

Sift together twice the all-purpose flour, cake flour, baking soda and salt.

Cream the butter in the large bowl of an electric mixer on low speed for 5 minutes, scraping down the sides of the bowl occasionally. Add the light brown sugar and granulated sugar; beat on moderate speed for 3 minutes. Scrape down the sides of the bowl with a rubber spatula to keep the mixture even-textured. Beat in the eggs, one at a time, blending well after each addition. Blend in the vanilla extract. On low speed, add the sifted mixture and mix until the particles of flour are absorbed. Stir in the chocolate chips.

For each batch, drop rounded tablespoon-size mounds of dough onto a lined sheet, spacing the mounds about 2 1/2 to 3 inches apart.

Bake the cookies for about 14 minutes, or until golden brown all over. To remain crisp, the cookies must bake to an *even* brown color. After 1 minute, transfer the cookies to cooling racks using a wide metal spatula. Cool completely.

Store in an airtight container.

VARIATION

For *Chocolate Chip Crisps with Walnuts, Pecans or Macadamia Nuts*, stir 1 cup coarsely chopped nuts into the batter along with the chocolate chips.

My Grandmother's
Oatmeal Chocolate Chip Cookies

◆ *about 4 dozen 3 1/2-inch cookies* ◆

*T*hese crisp-chewy cookies are ideal for gift-giving, for they highlight two popular ingredients, oats and chocolate chips. Occasionally, my grandmother Lilly would add flaked coconut to the dough along with the chocolate chips—a delicious variation.

*1 1/2 cups unsifted all-purpose
  flour
1 teaspoon baking soda
1/2 teaspoon salt
1/2 pound (2 sticks) unsalted
  butter, softened
3/4 cup granulated sugar
3/4 cup light brown sugar*

*2 extra-large eggs
1 teaspoon hot water
1 teaspoon vanilla extract
2 cups "quick-cooking" (not
  instant) rolled oats
1 12-ounce bag semisweet
  chocolate chips*

Preheat the oven to 375 degrees. Line two cookie sheets with lengths of parchment paper.

Sift together the flour, baking soda and salt.

Cream the butter in the large bowl of an electric mixer on low speed for 5 minutes. Add the granulated sugar and beat on moderately high speed for 2 minutes. Add the light brown sugar and beat for 2 minutes longer. Beat in the eggs, one at a time, blending well after each addition. Mix in the water and vanilla extract. On low speed, add the flour mixture and mix until the particles of flour are absorbed. Stir in the oats and chocolate chips.

For each batch, drop tablespoon-size mounds of dough onto a lined cookie sheet, spacing the mounds about 3 inches apart.

Bake the cookies for 12 minutes, or until golden and just set. After 1 minute, transfer the cookies to cooling racks using a wide metal spatula. Cool completely.

Store in an airtight container.

VARIATIONS

For *My Grandmother's Oatmeal Chocolate Chip Cookies with Coconut*, add 1 1/2 cups sweetened flaked coconut to the dough along with the oats and chocolate chips.

For *My Grandmother's Oatmeal Chocolate Chip Cookies with Walnuts*, add 1 cup chopped walnuts to the dough along with the oats and chocolate chips.

Soft Milk Chocolate Cookies

◆ about 2 1/2 dozen 3 1/2-to-4-inch cookies ◆

These soft drop cookies are loaded with coconut and craggy bits of milk chocolate.

1 3/4 cups plus 2 tablespoons
   unsifted all-purpose flour
1/4 cup plus 2 tablespoons unsifted
   cake flour
1/4 teaspoon cream of tartar
1/2 teaspoon salt
12 tablespoons (1 1/2 sticks)
   unsalted butter, softened
5 tablespoons shortening
3/4 cup granulated sugar
1/2 cup light brown sugar

1/4 cup dark brown sugar
1 extra-large egg
1 extra-large egg yolk
2 teaspoons vanilla extract
1/2 teaspoon almond extract
1 bar (7 ounces) milk chocolate,
   coarsely chopped
1 1/4 cups sweetened flaked
   coconut
2/3 cup chopped walnuts

Preheat the oven to 325 degrees. Line two cookie sheets with lengths of parchment paper.

Sift together the all-purpose flour, cake flour, cream of tartar and salt.

Cream the butter and shortening in the large bowl of an electric mixer on low speed for 5 minutes. Add the granulated sugar, light and dark brown sugars; beat for 3 minutes on moderate speed. Beat in the egg and egg yolk. Blend in the vanilla extract and almond extract. On low speed, add the sifted mixture and mix until the particles of flour are absorbed. Stir in the milk chocolate, coconut and walnuts.

For each batch, drop 2 tablespoon-size mounds of the dough onto a lined cookie sheet, spacing the mounds about 2 to 2 1/2 inches apart.

Bake the cookies for 15 minutes, or until a light golden color. After 1 minute, transfer the cookies to cooling racks using a wide metal spatula. Cool completely.

Store in an airtight container.

Nutmeg Sugar Tops

◆ *about 3 dozen 1 1/2-to-2-inch cookies* ◆

These cookies, quite buttery and delicate, are heavenly served with a baked or poached fruit compote. They keep nicely in an airtight tin for 2 weeks.

1 3/4 cups unsifted all-purpose flour
1 1/4 cups unsifted cake flour
1/4 teaspoon baking powder
1/8 teaspoon cream of tartar
1/8 teaspoon salt

1 3/4 teaspoons freshly grated nutmeg
3 sticks (3/4 pound) unsalted butter, softened
2/3 cup unsifted confectioners' sugar

TO FINISH THE COOKIES:
Ice-cold water, for brushing the cookies

Granulated sugar, for sprinkling on the cookies

Sift together the all-purpose flour, cake flour, baking powder, cream of tartar, salt and nutmeg.

Cream the butter in the large bowl of an electric mixer on low speed for 5 minutes. Add the confectioners' sugar and beat for 1 to 2 minutes on moderate speed. Blend in the sifted mixture on low speed. The dough will be quite sticky.

Place the dough on a large sheet of wax paper, place another sheet on top and roll out the dough to a thickness of about 1/3 inch. Carefully transfer the sheet of dough onto a cookie sheet and refrigerate until very firm, about

4 hours, or overnight, if you wish. (The sheet of dough can be stored in the refrigerator, well wrapped, for up to 2 days.)

Peel off the wax paper just before cutting the dough. Stamp out 1 1/2-to-1 3/4-inch rounds or squares and place them, 2 inches apart, on the lined cookie sheets. Lightly brush the tops of the cookies with cold water and sprinkle with granulated sugar. Reroll the scraps, refrigerate until firm and cut the remaining cookies.

Bake the cookies in a preheated 350-degree oven for 17 to 20 minutes, or until set. After 1 minute, transfer the cookies to cooling racks using a wide metal spatula. Cool completely.

Store in an airtight container.

Toffee Crunch Cookies

◆ *about 4 1/2 dozen 3 1/2-inch cookies* ◆

*C*risp and crunchy cookies, spiked with toasted almonds and chunks of chocolate-covered toffee candy.

2 3/4 cups unsifted all-purpose
    flour
1/4 cup unsifted cake flour
1 1/4 teaspoons salt
3/4 pound (3 sticks) unsalted
    butter, softened

1 1/3 cups granulated sugar
2 1/2 teaspoons vanilla extract
9 bars (1.4 ounces each)
    chocolate-covered almond toffee
    candy, cut into chunks
1 cup chopped almonds

Preheat the oven to 350 degrees. Line two cookie sheets with lengths of parchment paper.

Sift together the all-purpose flour, cake flour and salt.

Cream the butter in the large bowl of an electric mixer on low speed for 5 minutes. Add the sugar in two additions, beating for 2 minutes on moderate speed after each portion is added. Blend in the vanilla extract. On low speed, add the sifted mixture and mix until the particles of flour are absorbed. Stir in the toffee and almonds.

For each batch, drop heaping tablespoon-size mounds of dough onto a lined cookie sheet, spacing the mounds about 2 inches apart.

Bake the cookies for 15 minutes, or until golden. After 1 minute, transfer the cookies to cooling racks using a wide metal spatula. Cool completely.

Store in an airtight container.

Walnut and Coconut Bar Cookies

◆ 30 2 1/4-by-1 3/4-inch bar cookies ◆

*T*hese bars, thickset with nuts and coconut, are delicious served with hot coffee or iced tea.

1 cup unsifted all-purpose flour	*1 1/2 cups light brown sugar*
1/4 teaspoon baking powder	*1/3 cup granulated sugar*
1/2 teaspoon salt	*4 extra-large eggs*
1/4 teaspoon ground cinnamon	*1 teaspoon vanilla extract*
1/4 teaspoon freshly grated nutmeg	*1 1/2 cups chopped walnuts*
10 tablespoons (1 stick plus 2 tablespoons) unsalted butter, melted and cooled	*1 cup sweetened flaked coconut*

Preheat the oven to 350 degrees. Butter and flour a 13-by-9-by-2-inch baking pan.

Sift together the flour, baking powder, salt, cinnamon and nutmeg.

Whisk the butter, light brown sugar, granulated sugar and eggs in a bowl. Blend in the vanilla extract. Add the flour mixture and mix until the particles of flour are absorbed. Stir in the walnuts and coconut.

Pour and scrape the batter into the prepared pan. Bake for 25 minutes, or until just set.

Place the pan on a cooling rack. Cool completely. Cut into thirty 2 1/4-by-1 3/4-inch rectangles. Remove the bars from the pan using a metal spatula.

Store in an airtight container.

Date Squares

◆ *16 2-by-2-inch bar cookies* ◆

*T*he natural combination of dates and walnuts frequently appears in batters and doughs for American tea breads and drop cookies. The dates add a sweet and mellow richness, and the walnuts are a crunchy counterpoint to the chewy dates. In this recipe, they are paired in a bar cookie, with just enough flour, butter and eggs to bind. Date squares are a splendid sweet to pack up and give during the autumn or winter. These are one of my favorite bar cookies.

2/3 cup unsifted all-purpose flour
3 tablespoons unsifted whole wheat flour
1/2 teaspoon baking powder
1/4 teaspoon baking soda
1/2 teaspoon salt
1 teaspoon ground cinnamon
1/4 teaspoon freshly grated nutmeg
1/4 teaspoon ground cardamom
1/4 teaspoon ground allspice

4 tablespoons (1/2 stick) unsalted butter, melted and cooled
1/2 cup granulated sugar
1/4 cup light brown sugar
2 extra-large eggs
1 teaspoon vanilla extract
2 cups (10 ounces) chopped pitted dates
3/4 cup chopped walnuts

Preheat the oven to 350 degrees. Butter and flour an 8-by-8-by-2-inch baking pan.

Sift together the all-purpose flour, whole wheat flour, baking powder, baking soda, salt, cinnamon, nutmeg, cardamom and allspice into a large mixing bowl.

Whisk the butter, granulated sugar, light brown sugar, eggs and vanilla extract in a bowl.

Pour the sugar-egg mixture over the flour mixture and mix until the particles of flour are absorbed. Stir in the dates and walnuts.

Pour and scrape the batter into the prepared pan. Bake for 25 minutes, or until just set.

Place the pan on a cooling rack. Cool completely. Cut into 2-by-2-inch squares. Remove the squares from the pan using a metal spatula.

Store in an airtight container.

Plenty of Everything Fudgies

◆ *30 2 1/4-by-1 3/4-inch bar cookies* ◆

*H*ere you have brownies made excessive and extravagant by a jumble of nuts, chocolate chips and coconut—all intruding their way into a fudgy batter. I love them.

3/4 cup unsifted all-purpose flour
1/4 cup unsifted cake flour
2 tablespoons cornstarch
1/4 teaspoon baking powder
1/2 teaspoon salt
1/2 cup semisweet chocolate chips
1/2 pound (2 sticks) unsalted
   butter, melted and cooled
5 squares (5 ounces) unsweetened
   chocolate, melted and cooled

2 cups granulated sugar
4 extra-large eggs
1 1/2 teaspoons vanilla extract
3/4 cup chopped walnuts
3/4 cup chopped pecans
1/2 cup chopped Brazil nuts
1/2 cup raisins
1/2 cup sweetened shredded
   coconut

Preheat the oven to 325 degrees. Butter and flour a 13-by-9-by-2-inch baking pan.

Sift together the all-purpose flour, cake flour, cornstarch, baking powder and salt. Toss the chocolate chips with 1 teaspoon of the sifted mixture.

Whisk the butter and chocolate in a large mixing bowl. Blend in the sugar. Beat in the eggs and vanilla extract. Add the flour mixture and mix until the particles of flour are absorbed. Stir in the chocolate chips, walnuts, pecans, Brazil nuts, raisins and coconut.

Pour and scrape the batter into the prepared pan. Bake for 35 to 38 minutes, or until just set.

Place the pan on a cooling rack. Cool completely. Cut into thirty 2 1/4-by-1 3/4-inch rectangles. Remove the bars from the pan using a metal spatula.

Store in an airtight container.

Coconut and Macadamia Rusks

◆ *about 30 2 1/2-by-3 3/4-inch rusks* ◆

*T*his recipe is a variation of the *Cinnamon-Cashew "Dunking" Cookies* that appears in *Country Cookies: An Old-Fashioned Collection* (New York: Harper & Row, 1990), the third volume in my trilogy of country baking books. These are twice-baked cookies: In the first stage, the batter is baked in shallow metal ice cube trays (without the dividers). The resulting short loaf "cake" is cut into slices, arranged on cookie sheets, dusted with cinnamon-sugar and baked again—at a lower temperature—until firm through and through. The rusks are crisp yet tender, and ideal for serving with hot coffee or tea.

3/4 cup sweetened flaked coconut
1 1/2 cups finely chopped
    macadamia nuts
2 cups sifted all-purpose flour
1/4 cup unsifted cake flour
1 teaspoon baking powder
1/4 teaspoon salt

3/4 teaspoon ground cinnamon
3/4 teaspoon freshly grated nutmeg
3 extra-large eggs
1 cup granulated sugar
1 cup vegetable oil
1 1/2 teaspoons pure vanilla
    extract

TO FINISH THE RUSKS:

1/2 cup granulated sugar blended
    with 1 teaspoon ground
    cinnamon

Preheat the oven to 350 degrees. Remove the dividers from two 11-by-4-by-1 1/2-inch metal ice cube trays. Butter and flour the trays.

Process the coconut in the bowl of a food processor using the metal blade for 3 to 4 seconds. Mix the coconut with the macadamia nuts; set aside.

Resift the all-purpose flour with the cake flour, baking powder, salt, cinnamon and nutmeg.

Beat the eggs in the large bowl of an electric mixer on moderately high speed for 5 minutes. Add the sugar and continue beating for 3 to 4 minutes. Add the oil and vanilla extract, and continue beating for 3 minutes longer, or until the oil is incorporated into the egg and sugar mixture. Blend in the sifted mixture on low speed. Stir in the coconut–macadamia nut mixture.

Scrape the batter into the prepared pans, dividing it evenly between them.

Bake for 30 minutes, or until a wooden pick emerges from the center of each cake without any moist, clinging particles adhering to it.

Reduce the oven temperature to 275 degrees.

Cool each cake in the pan on a rack for 4 to 5 minutes, invert onto another rack and turn each right side up. Cool for 15 to 20 minutes.

Cut each cake into about fifteen 1/2-inch thick slices using a sharp serrated knife. Arrange the slices on two jellyroll pans or cookie sheets. Bake the slices for 10 minutes. Sprinkle a little cinnamon-sugar mixture over the top of the slices and continue baking for 10 to 15 minutes. Turn the slices over and sprinkle the tops with more cinnamon-sugar. Bake for 10 to 15 minutes more, or longer, until they are quite firm.

Remove the rusks to a cooling rack using a wide metal spatula. Cool completely.

Store in an airtight container.

(continued)

VARIATION

For *Coconut and Pecan Rusks*, substitute pecans for the macadamia nuts.

NOTE: An edge of each rusk can be partially dipped in melted chocolate, then when the chocolate is on the point of setting, a narrow band can be rimmed in chopped, toasted macadamia nuts (or pecans, if you are making the variation). Very pretty. To dip the cookies, refer to the method on page 35 in the recipe for *Mint Chocolate Rusks*.

Mint Chocolate Rusks

◆ *about 2 dozen 2-by-4-to-5-inch rusks* ◆

*O*ne holiday season not too long ago, I made a mountain of these rusks, dipped them in chocolate and mailed them out to food-loving friends. Upon tasting these crunchy rusks, my editor, Susan Friedland, persuaded me to include the recipe for them in this book. It is roughly based on the formula for *Coconut and Macadamia Rusks* on page 30, but uses butter instead of oil and a lavish amount of chocolate; the second baking of the cookies is completed at a higher temperature and for a shorter length of time than the rusks on page 30.

The baked rusks can be finished in one of two ways: dusted with granulated sugar while still warm, or partially dipped in a melted chocolate glaze. To dip them in chocolate, either you must master the technique of tempering chocolate or simply buy a good-quality glaze, which is created to dry firm and glossy. I use a glaze. Albert Uster Imports, Inc., sells a terrific glaze called Hard Dark Chocolate Glaze (catalog number C20320) and, once melted, is ideal for enrobing cookies (or fruit). As stated in the catalog, Albert Uster, Inc., can be contacted at three addresses: On the East Coast, 9211 Gaither Road, Gaithersburg, Maryland 20877 (301-258-7350); in the Midwest, 8600 NE Underground Drive, Pillar #131, Kansas City, Missouri 64161 (816-452-8047); in the West, 9845 Kitty Lane, Oakland, California 94603 (510-569-0280). In addition, you can telephone: 1-800-231-8154. The Hard Dark Chocolate Glaze comes in blocks that I cut into chunks and store, tightly covered, in a large jar.

Mint Chocolate Rusks keep marvelously in a covered tin for at least 2 weeks.

(continued)

1 1/3 cups unsifted all-purpose
    flour
1/3 cup unsifted cake flour
3 tablespoons cocoa
1 3/4 teaspoons baking powder
1/4 teaspoon baking soda
1/4 teaspoon salt
1 cup semisweet mint-flavored
    chocolate chips

8 tablespoons (1 stick) unsalted
    butter, softened
1 1/4 cups superfine sugar
3 extra-large eggs
1 tablespoon milk
2 teaspoons vanilla extract
4 ounces (4 squares) unsweetened
    chocolate, melted and cooled

TO FINISH THE RUSKS:

Granulated sugar, or, about 3/4
    pound chocolate glaze, melted
    and transferred to a bowl, for
    dipping the baked rusks

Preheat the oven to 350 degrees. Remove the dividers from two 11-by-4-by-1 1/2-inch metal ice cube trays. Butter and flour the trays.

Sift the all-purpose flour, cake flour, cocoa, baking powder, baking soda and salt. Toss the mint-flavored chocolate chips with 2 teaspoons of the sifted mixture.

Cream the butter in the large bowl of an electric mixer on low speed for 5 minutes. Add the sugar and continue beating for 3 to 4 minutes. Add the eggs, one at a time, beating well after each addition. Blend in the milk, vanilla extract and melted chocolate. Blend in the sifted mixture on low speed. Stir in the mint-flavored chocolate chips.

Scrape the batter into the prepared pans, dividing it evenly between them.

Bake for 25 minutes, or until a wooden pick emerges from the center of each cake without any clinging particles adhering to it.

Cool each cake in the pan on a rack for 3 to 4 minutes, invert onto another rack and turn each right side up. Cool for 10 to 15 minutes.

Leave the oven set at 350 degrees.

Cut each cake on the diagonal into about twelve 3/4-inch-thick slices, using a sharp serrated knife. Arrange the slices on two jellyroll pans or cookie sheets. Bake the slices for about 7 to 9 minutes, turn them over and continue baking for 7 to 9 minutes longer, or until the rusks are firm.

Remove the rusks to a cooling rack using a wide metal spatula. If you are finishing the cookies with granulated sugar, sprinkle some over each while they are warm. Cool completely.

If you are using the chocolate glaze, dust off any crumbs adhering to the cookies with a soft pastry brush. Dip an end of a rusk in the glaze and hold it until it stops dripping, gently rocking the cookie from side to side. When the chocolate is on the point of setting, carefully place each rusk on a length of parchment paper until the glaze firms up, about 20 minutes. (To embellish the cookies further, you can dip the tip end of the glazed rusk in chocolate sprinkles; do this just before you place it on the parchment paper.)

Peel away the glazed cookies from the parchment paper. Store in an airtight container.

· 4 ·

Muffins and Biscuits

Muffins and biscuits—those sweet or savory handfuls—are luscious quick breads that can be put together while the oven is preheating. In almost no time, you can have a splendid gift, fresh, redolent and ready to pack up in tins, baskets or colorful bags.

To vary the look of the finished gift, consider stamping out biscuits with a square, rectangular, oval or heart-shaped cutter, instead of the traditional round. Spoon muffin batter in smaller miniature muffin tins, or double the recipe and bake the batter in the larger Texas-size muffin tins. The *Blueberry Corn Muffins* (page 38) or *Raisin-Bran Muffins* (page 37), *Chocolate Chip–Banana Muffins* (page 40), *Whole Wheat–Oatmeal Muffins* (page 46), and *Raspberry Cream Muffins* (page 44) are all adjustable enough to bake in miniature- or jumbo-size pans. For the miniature muffins, decrease the baking time by about 5 to 7 minutes; for the jumbo muffins, increase the baking time by about 5 to 8 minutes. No matter what size you are baking, a toothpick inserted into the center of a fully baked muffin should withdraw without any particles of batter clinging to it.

All of the muffins and biscuits in this chapter reheat well: A small note mentioning that they can be warmed in a moderate oven (350 degrees) for 5 or 6 minutes would be helpful to the recipient.

Raisin-Bran Muffins

◆ about 14 2 3/4-inch muffins ◆

*T*hese bran muffins, loaded with raisins and nuts, are dense and husky. The applesauce and sour cream in the batter keep them moist.

1 cup unsifted all-purpose flour
1 teaspoon baking powder
3/4 teaspoon baking soda
1/4 teaspoon salt
2 teaspoons ground cinnamon
1 teaspoon freshly grated
   nutmeg
1/4 teaspoon ground allspice
2 1/2 cups bran (not bran cereal)
6 tablespoons (3/4 stick) unsalted
   butter, melted and cooled
2 tablespoons solid shortening,
   melted and cooled

1/3 cup light brown sugar
1/3 cup granulated sugar
1 extra-large egg
1 1/2 teaspoons vanilla extract
2 tablespoons light molasses
3 tablespoons plain unsweetened
   applesauce
1 cup sour cream
1/3 cup buttermilk
1 1/4 cups dark raisins
2/3 cup chopped walnuts

Preheat the oven to 400 degrees. Butter and flour 14 muffin cups measuring 2 3/4 inches in diameter by 1 3/8 inches deep.

Stir the flour, baking powder, baking soda, salt, cinnamon, nutmeg and allspice together in a large bowl. Stir in the bran.

Whisk the butter, shortening, light brown sugar, granulated sugar, egg, vanilla extract, molasses, applesauce, sour cream and buttermilk in a bowl. Pour the liquid mixture over the dry ingredients, add the raisins and walnuts, and stir to form a batter. *(continued)*

Divide the batter among the muffin cups, mounding it as you go. The batter will fill the cups.

Bake the muffins for 20 minutes, or until a wooden picked inserted into the center of a muffin emerges clean and dry.

Cool the muffins in the pans on a rack for 1 to 2 minutes. Carefully remove the muffins to another cooling rack. Cool completely.

Store in an airtight container.

Blueberry Corn Muffins

◆ *1 dozen 2 3/4-inch muffins* ◆

*F*or these rich corn muffins, I prefer to use a fine yellow cornmeal instead of the stone-ground variety. The muffins make a superb gift for bringing along to a summer house.

1 1/2 cups unsifted all-purpose
   flour
3/4 cup yellow cornmeal
1/4 cup granulated sugar
2 1/4 teaspoons baking powder
1/2 teaspoon salt
1/2 teaspoon freshly grated
   nutmeg

1 cup fresh blueberries, picked over
6 tablespoons (3/4 stick)
   unsalted butter, melted
   and cooled
6 tablespoons solid shortening,
   melted and cooled
3 extra-large eggs
6 tablespoons milk

Preheat the oven to 400 degrees. Butter and flour 12 muffin cups measuring 2 3/4 inches in diameter by 1 3/8 inches deep.

Sift together the flour, cornmeal, sugar, baking powder, salt and nutmeg into a large bowl. Toss the blueberries in 2 teaspoons of the sifted mixture.

Whisk the butter, shortening, eggs and milk in a bowl. Pour the liquid mixture onto the flour mixture and stir to form a batter, using a few quick strokes. Fold in the blueberries.

Spoon the batter into the muffin cups, filling each a generous three-quarters full.

Bake the muffins for 15 to 20 minutes, or until well risen and plump. A wooden pick inserted into the center of a baked muffin will emerge without any clinging particles of batter. (If you pierce a berry, the pick will be stained.)

Cool the muffins in the pan on a rack for 1 to 2 minutes. Carefully remove the muffins to another cooling rack. Cool completely.

Store in an airtight container.

Chocolate Chip–Banana Muffins

◆ *about 14 2 3/4-inch muffins* ◆

These toothsome muffins are a welcome sweet to serve with coffee or tea. Make them when you have very ripe bananas on hand.

*1 1/4 cups unsifted all-purpose
   flour
1/4 cup unsifted cake flour
1 teaspoon baking powder
1 teaspoon baking soda
1/2 teaspoon salt
3/4 cup miniature semisweet
   chocolate chips
7 tablespoons unsalted butter,
   softened*

*1/2 cup granulated sugar
2 tablespoons light brown sugar
1 extra-large egg
1 teaspoon vanilla extract
1/3 cup sour cream
1 1/4 cups mashed bananas (about
   3 medium)
1/2 cup buttermilk
1/3 cup chopped walnuts*

Preheat the oven to 375 degrees. Butter and flour 14 muffin cups measuring 2 3/4 inches in diameter by 1 3/8 inches deep.

Sift together the all-purpose flour, cake flour, baking powder, baking soda and salt. Toss the chocolate chips with 1 tablespoon of the sifted mixture.

Cream the butter in the large bowl of an electric mixer on moderately high speed for 2 to 3 minutes. Add the granulated sugar and beat for 2 minutes; add the light brown sugar and beat for a minute longer. Beat in the egg and vanilla extract. Beat in the sour cream, then the mashed bananas. On low speed, alternately add the sifted mixture in two additions with the buttermilk in one addition, beginning and ending with the sifted mixture. Stir in the chocolate chips and walnuts.

Spoon the batter into the muffin cups, filling each about three-quarters full.

Bake the muffins for 20 minutes, or until well risen and a wooden pick inserted into the center of a muffin emerges clean and dry. (While the pick might be tinted with chocolate, it will be free of any clinging particles of muffin batter.)

Cool the muffins in the pan on a rack for 1 to 2 minutes. Carefully remove the muffins to another cooling rack. Cool completely.

Store in an airtight container.

Pear Muffins

◆ *1 dozen 2 3/4-inch muffins* ◆

*A*s these muffins bake, the shreds of fruit virtually melt into the batter, keeping them nice and moist until the last one is eaten. Serve with whipped maple butter or preserves.

1 3/4 cups unsifted all-purpose flour	7 tablespoons unsalted butter, melted and cooled
1/4 cup whole wheat flour	2/3 cup light brown sugar
1 3/4 teaspoons baking powder	2 tablespoons granulated sugar
3/4 teaspoon baking soda	1 extra-large egg
1/4 teaspoon salt	1 1/2 teaspoons vanilla extract
1 1/2 teaspoons ground ginger	3/4 cup buttermilk
1/2 teaspoon freshly grated nutmeg	1 1/4 cups shredded ripe pears (about 3 large)
1/4 teaspoon ground allspice	1 tablespoon chopped crystallized ginger
1/2 cup dark raisins	

Preheat the oven to 400 degrees. Butter and flour 12 muffin cups measuring 2 3/4 inches in diameter by 1 3/8 inches deep.

Sift together the all-purpose flour, whole wheat flour, baking powder, baking soda, salt, ginger, nutmeg and allspice. Toss the raisins with 2 teaspoons of the sifted mixture.

Whisk the butter, light brown sugar, granulated sugar, egg, vanilla extract and buttermilk in a large bowl. Add the flour mixture and stir to form a batter, using a few quick strokes. Stir in the pears, chopped ginger and raisins.

Divide the batter among the muffin cups.

Bake the muffins for 17 to 20 minutes, or until plump and a wooden picked inserted into the center of a muffin emerges clean and dry.

Cool the muffins in the pan on a rack for 1 to 2 minutes. Carefully remove the muffins to another cooling rack. Cool completely.

Store in an airtight container.

VARIATION

For *Apple Muffins*, substitute 2 tart "cooking" apples for the pears and ground cinnamon for the ginger. Omit the crystallized ginger. Stir 1/2 cup dark raisins into the batter along with the shredded apples.

Raspberry Cream Muffins

◆ *2 dozen 2 3/4-inch muffins* ◆

*T*his recipe makes a big batch of delicate muffins: The batter is creamy textured, cakelike and especially fine grained. These muffins are a lush summertime bakery treat. In winter, frozen raspberries are a good substitute for the fresh; use them directly from the freezer without defrosting.

3 1/2 cups unsifted all-purpose
   flour
1/2 cup unsifted cake flour
1 tablespoon plus 1 teaspoon
   baking powder
3/4 teaspoon salt
3/4 teaspoon ground cinnamon
3/4 teaspoon freshly grated
   nutmeg

1 2/3 cups fresh red raspberries
10 tablespoons (1 stick plus
   2 tablespoons) unsalted
   butter, softened
2 tablespoons solid shortening
1 1/4 cups granulated sugar
4 extra-large eggs
2 teaspoons vanilla extract
1 1/3 cups light cream

TO FINISH THE MUFFINS: (OPTIONAL)
About 1/3 cup granulated sugar

Preheat the oven to 400 degrees. Butter and flour 24 muffin cups measuring 2 3/4 inches in diameter by 1 3/8 inches deep.

Sift together the all-purpose flour, cake flour, baking powder, salt, cinnamon and nutmeg. Carefully toss the raspberries with 2 teaspoons of the sifted mixture.

Cream the butter and shortening in the large bowl of an electric mixer on moderately high speed for 3 minutes. Add the sugar in three additions, beating for 1 minute after each portion is added. Beat in the eggs, one at a time, blending well after each addition. Beat in the vanilla extract. On low speed, alternately add the sifted mixture in three additions with the cream in two additions, beginning and ending with the sifted mixture. Fold in the raspberries.

Spoon the batter into the muffin cups, filling each about two-thirds full.

Bake the muffins for 18 minutes, or until well risen and a wooden pick inserted into the center of a muffin emerges clean and dry. (The pick may be tinted pink if you pierce a berry.)

Cool the muffins in the pans on a rack for 1 to 2 minutes. Carefully remove the muffins to another cooling rack. Sprinkle the tops of the muffins with the granulated sugar, if you wish. Cool completely.

Store in an airtight container.

Whole Wheat–Oatmeal Muffins

◆ *about 1 1/2 dozen 2 3/4-inch muffins* ◆

*T*hese are hearty muffins, coarse-textured and dense. Serve them for breakfast or brunch, with whole-fruit preserves.

2 1/3 cups "quick-cooking" (not instant) rolled oats

2 cups buttermilk

1 1/2 cups unsifted all-purpose flour

2/3 cup unsifted whole wheat flour

1 tablespoon plus 1/2 teaspoon baking powder

1 teaspoon baking soda

1/2 teaspoon salt

2 1/2 teaspoons ground cinnamon

1 teaspoon freshly grated nutmeg

1/4 teaspoon ground ginger

8 tablespoons (1 stick) unsalted butter, melted and cooled

4 tablespoons solid shortening, melted and cooled

1 cup less 2 tablespoons granulated sugar

2/3 cup light brown sugar

2 extra-large eggs

2 teaspoons vanilla extract

2/3 cup golden raisins

Preheat the oven to 400 degrees. Butter and flour 18 muffin cups measuring 2 3/4 inches in diameter by 1 3/8 inches deep.

Place the oats in a bowl, pour over the buttermilk, stir and let stand for 20 minutes.

Sift together the all-purpose flour, whole wheat flour, baking powder, baking soda, salt, cinnamon, nutmeg and ginger.

Whisk the butter, shortening, granulated sugar, light brown sugar, eggs and vanilla extract in a large bowl. Add the flour mixture and stir to form a batter, using a few quick strokes. Blend in the oats and raisins.

Divide the batter among the muffin cups.

Bake the muffins for 17 to 20 minutes, or until well risen and a wooden pick inserted into the center of a muffin emerges clean and dry.

Cool the muffins in the pans on a rack for 1 to 2 minutes. Carefully remove the muffins to another cooling rack. Cool completely.

Store in an airtight container.

Jumbo Prune Streusel Muffins

◆ *7 4-inch muffins* ◆

*F*illed with nuggets of chopped prunes and topped with a crumble of walnuts and sugar, these make pleasant breakfast muffins. The batter is fortified with two mashed bananas, which adds moistness and offsets the flavor of the prunes in an intriguing way.

FOR THE WALNUT STREUSEL:

1/3 cup light brown sugar
2 tablespoons unsalted butter, cut into bits
1/3 cup chopped walnuts

1 1/2 tablespoons unsifted all-purpose flour
1/4 teaspoon ground cinnamon

FOR THE MUFFIN BATTER:

2 cups unsifted all-purpose flour
1 1/4 teaspoons baking powder
3/4 teaspoon baking soda
1/4 teaspoon salt
1 1/4 teaspoons ground cinnamon
1/2 teaspoon freshly grated nutmeg
1 cup chopped moist pitted prunes
2 tablespoons solid shortening

6 tablespoons (3/4 stick) unsalted butter, softened
1/2 cup granulated sugar
1/3 cup light brown sugar
2 extra-large eggs
2 teaspoons vanilla extract
3 tablespoons sour cream
1 cup mashed bananas (about 2 medium)

Preheat the oven to 375 degrees. Butter and flour 7 muffin cups measuring a scant 4 inches in diameter by 1 3/4 inches deep.

For the streusel, blend together the light brown sugar, butter, walnuts, flour, and cinnamon with your fingertips until small, soft lumps are formed. Set aside.

Sift together the all-purpose flour, baking powder, baking soda, salt, cinnamon and nutmeg. Toss the prunes with 2 teaspoons of the sifted mixture.

Cream the shortening and butter in the large bowl of an electric mixer on moderately high speed for 2 to 3 minutes. Add the granulated sugar and light brown sugar, and continue beating for 2 minutes. Beat in the eggs, one at a time, blending well after each addition. Blend in the vanilla extract, sour cream and mashed bananas. Add the sifted mixture on low speed, beating until the particles of flour are absorbed. Stir in the prunes.

Divide the batter among the muffin cups. Sprinkle a little of the streusel on top of each muffin.

Bake the muffins for 20 minutes, or until golden. A wooden pick inserted into the center of a baked muffin will emerge without any clinging particles of batter. (If you run into a piece of prune, the pick may be stained.)

Cool the muffins in the pan on a rack for 1 to 2 minutes. Carefully remove the muffins to another cooling rack. Cool completely.

Store in an airtight container.

VARIATIONS

For *Jumbo Date-Pecan Streusel Muffins*, substitute 1/3 cup chopped pecans for the walnuts in the streusel mixture and 1 cup chopped pitted dates for the prunes in the muffin batter.

For *Jumbo Apricot Streusel Muffins*, substitute 1 cup chopped dried apricots for the prunes in the muffin batter.

Jumbo Chocolate Chip Cookie Muffins

◆ *1/2 dozen 4-inch muffins* ◆

*T*hese muffins will appeal to those who love the taste of chocolate chip cookies—that delectable combination of butter, chocolate chips, nuts and brown sugar.

1 2/3 cups unsifted all-purpose flour

1/3 cup plus 2 teaspoons unsifted cake flour

1 1/2 teaspoons baking powder

1/2 teaspoon baking soda

1/4 teaspoon salt

1 1/4 cups miniature semisweet chocolate chips

10 tablespoons (1 stick plus 2 tablespoons) unsalted butter, softened

3/4 cup light brown sugar

1 extra-large egg

1 square (1 ounce) unsweetened chocolate, melted and cooled

2 teaspoons vanilla extract

1/2 cup plus 1 tablespoon half-and-half, blended with 1 teaspoon lemon juice

3/4 cup chopped pecans

Preheat the oven to 375 degrees. Butter and flour 6 jumbo muffin cups measuring a scant 4 inches in diameter by 1 3/4 inches deep.

Sift together the all-purpose flour, cake flour, baking powder, baking soda and salt. Toss the chocolate chips with 1 tablespoon of the sifted mixture.

Cream the butter in the large bowl of an electric mixer on moderately high speed for 2 to 3 minutes. Add the sugar and beat for 3 minutes. Beat in the egg. Blend in the melted chocolate and vanilla extract. On low speed, alternately add the sifted mixture in two additions with the half-and-half in one addition, beginning and ending with the sifted mixture. Stir in the chocolate chips and pecans.

Divide the batter among the muffin cups.

Bake the muffins for 29 to 30 minutes, or until well risen and a wooden pick inserted into the center of a muffin emerges clean and dry. (While the pick may be tinted with chocolate, it should be free of any unbaked particles of muffin batter.)

Cool the muffins in the pan on a rack for 1 to 2 minutes. Carefully remove the muffins to another cooling rack. Cool completely.

Store in an airtight container.

VARIATIONS

For *Jumbo Butterscotch Chip Muffins*, substitute butterscotch-flavored chips for the semisweet chocolate chips and chopped walnuts for the pecans.

For *Jumbo Milk Chocolate Chip Muffins*, substitute milk chocolate chips for the semisweet chocolate chips.

For *Jumbo White Chocolate Chip Muffins*, substitute white chocolate chips for the semisweet chocolate chips.

For *Bittersweet Chocolate Chunk Muffins with Walnuts and Pecans*, substitute 3 3-ounce bars bittersweet chocolate, chopped, for the semisweet chocolate chips; use 1/2 cup chopped walnuts and 1/2 cup chopped pecans.

NOTE: For a special treat, the tops of the baked muffins can be lightly coated with a chocolate glaze, such as the glaze used for dipping the rusks on page 33. Drizzle the melted glaze over the cooled muffins.

Tender Buttermilk Biscuits

◆ *about 10 2 1/2-inch biscuits* ◆

*B*iscuits made with buttermilk are soft and delicate, and just made for serving with roasted chicken and pan gravy, fried chicken or country ham.

1 3/4 cups unsifted all-purpose
   flour
1/4 cup unsifted cake flour
1 1/2 teaspoons baking powder
1 1/2 teaspoons baking soda

1 teaspoon salt
2 tablespoons granulated sugar
2/3 cup solid shortening
2/3 cup plus 1 tablespoon
   buttermilk

Preheat the oven to 425 degrees. Butter and flour a cookie sheet or jelly-roll pan.

Thoroughly combine the all-purpose flour, cake flour, baking powder, baking soda, salt and sugar in a large mixing bowl. Add the shortening and, using two round-bladed knives, cut into small lumps. With your fingertips, reduce the lumps to small bits, rubbing them into the flour mixture. Blend in the buttermilk with a few quick strokes. Knead the dough in the bowl a few times.

Place the dough on a lightly floured work surface. Roll out or pat the dough until it is a generous 1/2 inch thick. Stamp out rounds of dough using a plain 2-inch round cutter. Place the biscuits on the baking pan, spacing them about 1 inch apart.

Bake the biscuits for 15 minutes, or until golden. Transfer the pan of biscuits to a cooling rack and let stand for 1 minute. Remove the biscuits to another cooling rack using a wide spatula. Cool completely.

Store in an airtight container.

Cheese Drop Biscuits

◆ *about 14 3-inch biscuits* ◆

*T*hese biscuits, made with Cheddar cheese and sour cream, are rich and satisfying. Serve them with a chili-based stew, chicken fricassee or chowder.

2 cups unsifted all-purpose flour
1 3/4 teaspoons baking powder
3/4 teaspoon baking soda
1/4 teaspoon cream of tartar
1 teaspoon salt
1/4 teaspoon cayenne pepper,
 or to taste

2 tablespoons granulated sugar
1/3 cup solid shortening
3 tablespoons unsalted butter, cold
1 cup sour cream, at room
 temperature
2/3 cup shredded Cheddar cheese

Preheat the oven to 425 degrees. Butter and flour a cookie sheet or jelly-roll pan.

Thoroughly mix the flour, baking powder, baking soda, cream of tartar, salt, cayenne pepper and sugar in a large mixing bowl. Add the shortening and butter and, using two round-bladed knives, cut the fat into the flour until reduced to small lumps. With your fingertips, reduce the lumps to small bits, rubbing them into the flour mixture. Blend in the sour cream and cheese with a few quick strokes.

Drop heaping tablespoon mounds of dough onto the baking pan, spacing them about 2 inches apart.

Bake the biscuits for 15 minutes, or until firm, set and golden. Transfer the pan of biscuits to a cooling rack and let stand for 1 minute. Remove the biscuits to another cooling rack using a wide spatula. Cool completely.

Store in an airtight container.

Spiced Pecan Drop Biscuits

◆ *about 14 3-inch biscuits* ◆

*C*raggy on the outside and tender textured within, these biscuits are wonderful served at breakfast or brunch. As they are rather moist, the biscuits can be baked ahead, frozen and reheated.

2 3/4 cups unsifted all-purpose
    flour
1/4 cup unsifted cake flour
1 tablespoon baking powder
1 teaspoon baking soda
1/2 teaspoon cream of tartar
1 1/2 teaspoons salt
1 tablespoon ground cinnamon
1 1/2 teaspoons freshly grated
    nutmeg

3/4 teaspoon ground ginger
1/4 teaspoon ground allspice
1/4 cup plus 1 tablespoon
    granulated sugar
3/4 cup solid shortening
1 1/2 cups buttermilk
2/3 cup chopped pecans
2/3 cup dark raisins

Preheat the oven to 425 degrees. Butter and flour a cookie sheet or jelly-roll pan.

Thoroughly mix the all-purpose flour, cake flour, baking powder, baking soda, cream of tartar, salt, cinnamon, nutmeg, ginger, allspice and sugar in a large mixing bowl. Add the shortening and, using two round-bladed knives, cut into small lumps. With your fingertips, reduce the lumps to small bits, rubbing them into the flour mixture. Blend in the buttermilk, pecans and raisins with a few quick strokes.

Drop heaping tablespoon mounds of dough onto the baking pan, spacing them about 2 inches apart.

Bake the biscuits for 15 minutes, or until firm and golden. Transfer the pan of biscuits to a cooling rack and let stand for 1 minute. Remove the biscuits to another cooling rack using a wide spatula. Cool completely.

Store in an airtight container.

· 5 ·

Loaf Cakes and
Tea Cakes

Soft-textured cakes, baked in standard-size loaf pans, emerge from the oven plump and full of flavor. Loaf cakes are easy gifts to pack up, for they can be wrapped neatly in clear, food-safe plastic wrap or cellophane and tucked into a basket or gift bag. These cakes are ideal to bring as a weekend treat if you are a houseguest or as your contribution to a bring-a-dish supper.

All of the cakes can be enjoyed as is, topped only by a sprinkling of confectioners' sugar, but most of them are even more delicious served with a fresh fruit compote and pouf of whipped cream. For example, the *Blueberry Tea Cake* (page 58) becomes a special dessert when sliced and served with a fresh blueberry compote on the side; homemade applesauce is an excellent complement for slices of *Spiced Whole Wheat Pumpkin Loaf* (page 66); and sliced apples, sautéed in a bit of butter and moistened with apple cider, is an ideal companion for fingers of *Applesauce Loaf Cake* (page 57). These cakes also shine at teatime, sliced and served as is with hot cups of lemon tea or tall glasses of iced tea.

Applesauce Loaf Cake

◆ *1 loaf, serving 6 to 8* ◆

*T*his spiced loaf is good to have in the house—as a breakfast cake, served with apple butter, or as dessert, accompanied by stewed fruit or baked apples doused with a little cider or rum.

1 1/2 cups unsifted all-purpose
   flour
1/3 cup unsifted cake flour
1 3/4 teaspoons baking powder
1/2 teaspoon baking soda
1/4 teaspoon salt
1 3/4 teaspoons ground cinnamon
1/4 teaspoon ground allspice
1/4 teaspoon ground ginger
1/8 teaspoon ground cardamom
3/4 cup dark raisins

8 tablespoons (1 stick) unsalted
   butter, softened
1/2 cup light brown sugar
1/3 cup granulated sugar
2 extra-large eggs
1 tablespoon light molasses
1 teaspoon vanilla extract
3/4 cup plain unsweetened
   applesauce
3 tablespoons sour cream
1/2 cup chopped walnuts

Preheat the oven to 350 degrees. Butter and flour a 9-by-5-by-3-inch loaf pan.

Sift together the all-purpose flour, cake flour, baking powder, baking soda, salt, cinnamon, allspice, ginger and cardamom. Toss the raisins with 2 teaspoons of the sifted mixture.

Cream the butter in the large bowl of an electric mixer on moderate speed for 3 minutes. Add the light brown sugar and beat for 2 minutes; add the granulated sugar and beat for 2 minutes longer. Beat in the eggs, one at a time, blending well after each addition. Beat in the molasses and vanilla extract. Blend in the applesauce and sour cream. The mixture will look slightly curdled. Add the sifted ingredients on low speed, mixing until the particles of flour are absorbed. Stir in the raisins and walnuts.

Pour and scrape the batter into the prepared pan. Bake the cake for 45 to 50 minutes, or until a wooden pick inserted into the loaf emerges clean and dry.

Cool the cake in the pan on a rack for 2 to 3 minutes, invert onto another rack and turn rightside up. Cool completely.

Store in an airtight container.

Blueberry Tea Cake

◆ *1 loaf, serving 6 to 8* ◆

*P*lump blueberries dot each slice of this light, fine-grained loaf cake. On a sultry summer afternoon, cut the cake into thick slices and serve with a pitcher of lemonade.

2 cups unsifted all-purpose flour
1 teaspoon baking powder
1/2 teaspoon baking soda
1/4 teaspoon salt
1/2 teaspoon freshly grated nutmeg
1/2 teaspoon ground cinnamon
1 cup fresh blueberries, picked over

8 tablespoons (1 stick) unsalted
  butter, softened
3/4 cup superfine sugar
2 extra-large eggs
1 teaspoon vanilla extract
1/4 cup sour cream

Preheat the oven to 350 degrees. Butter and flour a 9-by-5-by-3-inch loaf pan.

Sift together the all-purpose flour, baking powder, baking soda, salt, nutmeg and cinnamon. Toss the blueberries with 1 tablespoon of the sifted mixture.

Cream the butter in the large bowl of an electric mixer on moderately high speed for 3 minutes. Add the sugar and beat for 2 minutes. Beat in the eggs, one at a time, blending well after each addition. Beat in the vanilla extract. On low speed, add half of the sifted ingredients, the sour cream, then the balance of the sifted ingredients, mixing until the particles of flour are absorbed. Stir in the blueberries.

Pour and scrape the batter into the prepared pan. Bake the loaf for 55 minutes to 1 hour, or until nicely risen and a wooden pick inserted into the loaf emerges clean and dry. The baked loaf will pull away slightly from the sides of the pan.

Cool the loaf in the pan on a rack for 3 to 4 minutes, invert onto another rack and turn rightside up. Cool completely.

Store in an airtight container.

Chocolate Chunk
and Walnut Tea Cake

◆ *1 loaf, serving 6 to 8* ◆

*S*erve thick slices of this cake with tea or coffee, hot or iced. It's sure to appeal to anyone who loves chocolate chip cookies.

1 1/4 cups unsifted all-purpose flour

1/4 cup plus 2 tablespoons unsifted cake flour

1 teaspoon baking powder

1/4 teaspoon salt

2 bars (3 ounces each) bittersweet bar chocolate (such as Lindt "Excellence" or Tobler "Tradition"), cut into small chunks

3/4 cup chopped walnuts

8 tablespoons (1 stick) unsalted butter, softened

3/4 cup granulated sugar

1/4 cup light brown sugar

2 extra-large eggs

1 teaspoon vanilla extract

2/3 cup milk

Preheat the oven to 350 degrees. Butter and flour a 9-by-5-by-3-inch loaf pan.

Sift together the all-purpose flour, cake flour, baking powder and salt. Toss the chocolate chunks and walnuts with 1 tablespoon of the sifted mixture.

Cream the butter in the large bowl of an electric mixer on moderate speed for 3 minutes. Add the granulated sugar and beat on moderately high speed for 2 minutes. Add the light brown sugar and continue beating for 1 minute longer. Beat in the eggs, one at a time, blending well after each addition. Beat in the vanilla extract. On low speed, add half of the sifted ingredients, the milk, then the balance of the sifted ingredients, mixing just until the particles of flour are absorbed. Stir in the chocolate chunks and walnuts.

Pour and scrape the batter into the prepared pan. Bake the cake for 55 minutes to 1 hour, or until nicely risen and a wooden pick inserted into the cake emerges clean and dry. The baked cake will pull away slightly from the sides of the pan.

Cool the cake in the pan on a rack for 3 to 4 minutes, invert onto another rack and turn rightside up. Cool completely.

Store in an airtight container.

Date-Nut Tea Loaf

◆ *1 loaf, serving 6 to 8* ◆

*E*ach slice of this traditional tea cake is loaded with dates and walnuts. While the ingredients in this loaf are similar to those in the *Prune and Pecan Tea Loaf* on page 70, its texture is denser, with a more compact "crumb," and the brown sugar flavor is more distinct. Thinly sliced, it's a perfect match for freshly brewed coffee or tea.

2 cups unsifted all-purpose flour
1 teaspoon baking powder
1/2 teaspoon baking soda
1/4 teaspoon salt
1 teaspoon ground cinnamon
1/2 teaspoon freshly grated nutmeg
1/4 teaspoon ground allspice
2 cups (10 ounces) chopped pitted
   dates

8 tablespoons (1 stick) unsalted
   butter, softened
1/2 cup light brown sugar
2 extra-large eggs
1 1/2 teaspoons vanilla extract
1/3 cup buttermilk
3/4 cup chopped walnuts or pecans

Preheat the oven to 350 degrees. Butter and flour a 9-by-5-by-3-inch loaf pan.

Sift together the all-purpose flour, baking powder, baking soda, salt, cinnamon, nutmeg and allspice. Place the dates in a bowl, sprinkle them with 1 tablespoon of the sifted mixture and mix, coating the dates as evenly as possible. (The dates, if they are very soft, will clump together—just stir the flour in and around, separating the nuggets as you go.)

Cream the butter in the large bowl of an electric mixer on moderate speed for 3 minutes. Add the sugar and beat on moderately high speed for 2 minutes. Beat in the eggs, one at a time, blending well after each addition. Beat in the vanilla extract. On low speed, add half of the sifted ingredients, the buttermilk, then the balance of the sifted ingredients, mixing until the particles of flour are absorbed. Stir in the dates and walnuts or pecans.

Pour and scrape the batter into the prepared pan. Bake the cake for 1 hour, or until a wooden pick inserted into the cake emerges clean and dry. The baked cake will pull away slightly from the sides of the pan.

Cool the cake in the pan on a rack for 4 to 5 minutes, invert onto another rack and turn rightside up. Cool completely.

Store in an airtight container.

Shredded Carrot, Sour Cream and Raisin Loaves

◆ *4 loaves, each serving 3 to 4* ◆

*T*hese small, lightly sweetened loaves are reminiscent of carrot cake. Wrapped in clear cellophane and tied with a colorful ribbon, they would make a superb host or hostess gift.

1 cup unsifted all-purpose flour
1 cup unsifted cake flour
1/3 cup unsifted whole wheat flour
1/3 cup yellow cornmeal
1 1/4 teaspoons baking soda
1 teaspoon baking powder
1/2 teaspoon salt
1 1/2 teaspoons ground cinnamon
1/2 teaspoon ground ginger
1/4 teaspoon ground allspice
1/4 teaspoon ground cardamom

1 1/3 cups dark raisins
1/3 cup chopped walnuts
8 tablespoons (1 stick) unsalted
  butter, softened
1 cup granulated sugar
2 extra-large eggs
2 teaspoons vanilla extract
1 1/4 cups sour cream
1 3/4 cups peeled, shredded carrots
  (about 4 medium carrots)

Preheat the oven to 375 degrees. Butter and flour four 5-by-3-by-2 3/4-inch loaf pans.

Sift together the all-purpose flour, cake flour, whole wheat flour, cornmeal, baking soda, baking powder, salt, cinnamon, ginger, allspice and cardamom. Toss the raisins and walnuts with 2 teaspoons of the sifted mixture.

Cream the butter in the large bowl of an electric mixer on moderate speed for 5 minutes. Add the sugar and beat on moderately high speed for 3 minutes. Beat in the eggs, one at a time, blending well after each addition. Blend in the vanilla extract. On low speed, alternately add the sifted mixture in three additions with the sour cream in two additions, beginning and ending with the sifted mixture. Stir in the carrots, raisins and walnuts.

Pour and scrape the batter into the prepared pans, dividing it evenly among them. Bake the loaves for 40 to 45 minutes, or until a wooden pick inserted into each loaf emerges clean and dry. A baked loaf will pull away slightly from the sides of the pan.

Cool the loaves in the pans on a rack for 3 to 4 minutes, invert onto another rack and turn each rightside up. Cool completely.

Store in airtight containers.

Spiced Whole Wheat Pumpkin Loaf

◆ *1 loaf, serving 4 to 6* ◆

*T*his loaf, warmed to bring out the aroma of the spices and cut into thick fingers, is a fine addition to the tea table. Or nestle pieces in the Thanksgiving bread basket, along with corn muffins and yeast-raised rolls. Sometimes I give miniature versions of this tea bread as take-home presents to guests who drop by during the winter holidays.

1 cup unsifted all-purpose flour
1/2 cup unsifted whole wheat flour
1/2 teaspoon baking soda
1/2 teaspoon baking powder
1/4 teaspoon salt
1 teaspoon ground cinnamon
1/2 teaspoon ground ginger
1/2 teaspoon freshly grated nutmeg
3/4 cup dark raisins
3/4 cup chopped pitted dates

1/2 cup chopped walnuts
8 tablespoons (1 stick) unsalted
   butter, softened
3/4 cup light brown sugar
1 1/2 teaspoons pure vanilla
   extract
2 extra-large eggs
3/4 cup canned pumpkin (not
   pumpkin pie filling)

Preheat the oven to 350 degrees. Butter and flour an 8-by-4-by-3-inch loaf pan.

Sift together the all-purpose flour, whole wheat flour, baking soda, baking powder, salt, cinnamon, ginger and nutmeg. Toss the raisins, dates and walnuts with 1 tablespoon of the sifted mixture.

Cream the butter in the large bowl of an electric mixer on moderate speed for 5 minutes. Add the sugar and beat on moderately high speed for 2 minutes. Blend in the vanilla extract. Beat in the eggs, one at a time, blending well after each addition. Beat in the pumpkin. The mixture will look curdled. On low speed, add the sifted ingredients, mixing until the particles of flour are absorbed. Stir in the raisin-date-walnut mixture.

Pour and scrape the batter into the prepared pan. Bake the loaf for 50 to 55 minutes, or until a wooden pick inserted into each loaf emerges clean and dry. The baked loaf will pull away slightly from the sides of the pan.

Cool the loaf in the pan on a rack for 3 to 4 minutes, invert onto another rack and turn rightside up. Cool completely.

Store in an airtight container.

Banana Tea Cakes with Dried Fruit

◆ 4 loaves, each serving 3 to 4 ◆

*L*ittle loaves filled with currants, dates and prunes make good bread-and-butter gifts at Christmas.

1 3/4 cups unsifted all-purpose flour	3/4 cup diced pitted prunes
1/2 cup whole wheat flour	8 tablespoons (1 stick) unsalted butter, softened
1 1/2 teaspoons baking powder	1/2 cup light brown sugar
3/4 teaspoon baking soda	1/4 cup granulated sugar
1/4 teaspoon salt	2 extra-large eggs
1/2 teaspoon ground cinnamon	1 teaspoon vanilla extract
1/2 teaspoon freshly grated nutmeg	1 1/4 cups mashed ripe bananas (about 3 medium)
3/4 cup moist dried currants	1/2 cup buttermilk
3/4 cup chopped pitted dates	

Preheat the oven to 350 degrees. Butter and flour four 5-by-3-by-2 3/4-inch loaf pans.

Sift together the all-purpose flour, whole wheat flour, baking powder, baking soda, salt, cinnamon and nutmeg. Toss the currants, dates and prunes with 1 1/2 tablespoons of the sifted mixture.

Cream the butter in the large bowl of an electric mixer on moderate speed for 3 minutes. Add the light brown sugar and beat for 1 minute on moderately high speed. Add the granulated sugar and continue beating for 2 minutes longer. Beat in the eggs, one at a time, blending well after each addition. Beat in the vanilla extract and bananas. On low speed, add half of the sifted ingredients, the buttermilk, then the balance of the sifted ingredients, mixing until the particles of flour are absorbed. Stir in the currants, dates and prunes.

Pour and scrape the batter into the prepared pans, dividing it evenly among them. Bake the cakes for 40 minutes, or until a wooden pick inserted into each loaf emerges clean and dry.

Cool the cakes in the pans on a rack for 2 to 3 minutes, invert onto another rack and turn rightside up. Cool completely.

Store in airtight containers.

Prune and Pecan Tea Loaf

◆ *1 loaf, serving 6 to 8* ◆

A mosaic of diced prunes and chopped pecans decorates each slice of this moist loaf. It's especially nice to give during the autumn and winter months.

1 1/2 cups unsifted all-purpose flour
1/2 cup unsifted cake flour
1 teaspoon baking powder
3/4 teaspoon baking soda
1/4 teaspoon salt
1/4 teaspoon ground ginger
1/4 teaspoon ground allspice
4 tablespoons (1/2 stick) unsalted butter, softened

2 tablespoons solid shortening
1/2 cup light brown sugar
1/4 cup granulated sugar
2 extra-large eggs
1 teaspoon vanilla extract
1/2 cup plus 2 tablespoons buttermilk
1 1/2 cups chopped pitted prunes
2/3 cup chopped pecans

Preheat the oven to 350 degrees. Butter and flour a 9-by-5-by-3-inch loaf pan.

Sift together the all-purpose flour, cake flour, baking powder, baking soda, salt, ginger and allspice.

Cream the butter and shortening in the large bowl of an electric mixer on moderately high speed for 2 minutes. Add the light brown sugar and beat for 2 minutes; add the granulated sugar and beat for 2 minutes longer. Beat in the eggs, one at a time, blending well after each addition. Beat in the vanilla extract. On low speed, alternately add the sifted mixture in three additions with the buttermilk in two additions, beginning and ending with the sifted mixture. Stir in the prunes and pecans.

Pour and scrape the batter into the prepared pan. Bake the loaf for 50 to 55 minutes, or until plump and a wooden pick inserted into the loaf emerges clean and dry. The baked loaf will pull slightly from the sides of the baking pan.

Cool the bread in the pan on a rack for 3 to 4 minutes, invert onto another rack, and turn rightside up. Cool completely.

Store in an airtight container.

· 6 ·

"Keeping" Cakes

"K eeping" cakes stay moist and appealing, which makes them ideal for gift-giving. For the most part, the batters are silky and generously flavored with spices or fortified with chopped or pureed fruit, nuts, spirits, coconut or grated citrus peel. They are delicious on their own, served with a hot or cold beverage, or can be paired with a fresh or dried fruit compote, scoops of ice cream or a sweet dessert sauce.

Plain "keeping" cakes can be capped with a thin glaze made by combining citrus juice and granulated sugar. For this, mix 3 tablespoons lemon, orange or tangerine juice with 3 tablespoons granulated sugar and spoon over the top of the cake while it is warm. The glaze will be absorbed into the cake, adding a sweet-tart flavor.

Lemon Keeping Cake

◆ *1 cake, serving 16* ◆

A plain lemon cake, golden and delicately flavored. Serve thin slices with blueberries or strawberries and cream.

3 cups unsifted all-purpose flour	3 cups superfine sugar
1/2 teaspoon baking soda	6 eggs
1/2 teaspoon salt	2 teaspoons grated lemon peel
1/2 pound (2 sticks) unsalted butter, softened	2 teaspoons lemon extract
	1 cup sour cream
4 tablespoons solid shortening	1/4 cup milk

Preheat the oven to 325 degrees. Butter and flour a 10-inch tube pan.

Sift together the all-purpose flour, baking soda and salt.

Cream the butter and shortening in the large bowl of an electric mixer on moderate speed for 4 minutes. Add the sugar in three additions, beating on moderately high speed for 2 minutes after each portion is added. Beat in the eggs, one at a time, blending well after each addition. Beat in the lemon peel and lemon extract. On low speed, alternately add the sifted ingredients in three additions with the sour cream in two additions, beginning and ending with the sifted mixture. Blend in the milk.

Pour and scrape the batter into the prepared pan. Bake the cake for 1 hour and 20 minutes to 1 hour and 30 minutes, until golden and a wooden pick inserted into the cake emerges clean and dry.

Cool the cake in the pan on a rack for 5 minutes, invert the cake onto another cooling rack and turn rightside up. Cool completely.

Store in an airtight container.

Banana Gingerbread

◆ *1 loaf, serving 6 to 8* ◆

*T*his banana cake, scented with ginger and a medley of other aromatic spices, slices beautifully and is wonderful to have on hand for weekend guests. The combination of sour cream and mashed bananas keeps the loaf moist.

2 cups unsifted all-purpose flour
1 1/4 teaspoons baking powder
1/4 teaspoon baking soda
1/4 teaspoon salt
2 1/2 teaspoons ground ginger
1 teaspoon ground cinnamon
1/2 teaspoon freshly grated nutmeg
1/4 teaspoon ground allspice
1/4 teaspoon ground cloves
3/4 cup dark raisins

6 tablespoons (3/4 stick) unsalted
* butter, softened*
2 tablespoons solid shortening
2/3 cup light brown sugar
2 extra-large eggs
1/4 cup light molasses
1 1/2 teaspoons vanilla extract
1 1/4 cups mashed ripe bananas
* (about 3 medium)*
1/4 cup sour cream

Preheat the oven to 350 degrees. Butter and flour a 9-by-5-by-3-inch loaf pan.

Sift together the flour, baking powder, baking soda, salt, ginger, cinnamon, nutmeg, allspice and cloves. Toss the raisins with 2 teaspoons of the sifted mixture.

Cream the butter and shortening in the large bowl of an electric mixer on moderate speed for 3 minutes. Add the sugar and beat for 3 minutes. Beat in the eggs, one at a time, blending well after each addition. Beat on high speed for 1 minute. Blend in the molasses and vanilla extract. Beat in the mashed bananas and sour cream. Add the sifted ingredients on low speed, mixing until the particles of flour are absorbed. Stir in the raisins.

Pour and scrape the batter into the prepared pan. Bake the cake for 55 minutes to 1 hour, or until a wooden pick inserted into the cake emerges clean and dry.

Cool the cake in the pan on a rack for 3 to 4 minutes, invert onto another cooling rack and turn rightside up. Cool completely.

Store in an airtight container.

Honey Spice Cake

◆ *1 cake, serving 8* ◆

A cake such as this one, spiked with a bevy of spices and sweetened with both honey and dark brown sugar, should be baked for its aroma alone. It will perfume the kitchen. And once cut into squares and topped with a sprinkling of confectioners' sugar, the cake will grace your morning coffee break or afternoon tea.

2 cups unsifted all-purpose flour
3 tablespoons unsifted whole wheat
  flour
1 teaspoon baking powder
1/2 teaspoon salt
2 1/2 teaspoons ground cinnamon
1 1/2 teaspoons ground ginger
1 teaspoon freshly grated nutmeg
1/2 teaspoon ground allspice
1/4 teaspoon ground cloves
1/4 teaspoon ground cardamom
3/4 cup moist dried currants
1/2 cup chopped glazed apricots
  (about 4 large apricots)

10 tablespoons (1 stick plus
  2 tablespoons) unsalted butter,
  softened
3/4 cup dark brown sugar
1/4 cup granulated sugar
3 extra-large eggs
1 extra-large egg yolk
2 teaspoons grated orange peel
1 1/2 teaspoons vanilla extract
1/2 cup honey
1/3 cup heavy cream
2 tablespoons sour cream
1/2 cup chopped walnuts

Preheat the oven to 350 degrees. Butter and flour a 9-by-9-by-2-inch baking pan.

Sift together the all-purpose flour, whole wheat flour, baking powder, salt, cinnamon, ginger, nutmeg, allspice, cloves and cardamom. Toss the currants and apricots with 1 tablespoon of the sifted mixture.

Cream the butter in the large bowl of an electric mixer on moderate speed for 3 minutes. Add the dark brown sugar and beat for 2 minutes on moderately high speed; add the granulated sugar and continue beating for 2 minutes longer. Beat in the eggs, one at a time, blending well after each addition. Beat in the egg yolk, orange peel and vanilla extract. Blend in the honey. On low speed, add half of the sifted ingredients, the heavy cream and sour cream, then the balance of the sifted ingredients. Stir in the currants, apricots and walnuts.

Pour and scrape the batter into the prepared pan. Bake the cake for 50 to 55 minutes, until a wooden pick inserted into the cake emerges clean and dry. The baked cake will pull away slightly from the sides of the pan.

Cool the cake in the pan on a rack for 5 minutes, invert the cake onto another cooling rack and turn rightside up. Cool completely.

Store in an airtight container.

Maple-Pumpkin Keeping Cake

◆ *1 cake, serving 6 to 8* ◆

A few spoonfuls of maple syrup add depth to this cake batter, which is lightly flavored with cinnamon and nutmeg. Serve the cake with poached pears, homemade applesauce or warm sautéed apple slices.

2 cups unsifted all-purpose flour
1 teaspoon baking powder
1 teaspoon baking soda
1/2 teaspoon salt
1 1/4 teaspoons ground cinnamon
1/2 teaspoon freshly grated nutmeg
1/2 cup moist dried currants
8 tablespoons (1 stick) unsalted
    butter, softened

1 cup granulated sugar
2 extra-large eggs
1/2 teaspoon vanilla extract
1 1/4 cups canned pumpkin
    (not pumpkin pie filling)
1/4 cup plus 1 tablespoon sour
    cream
2 tablespoons maple syrup

Preheat the oven to 350 degrees. Butter and flour a 9-by-5-by-3-inch loaf pan.

Sift together the flour, baking powder, baking soda, salt, cinnamon and nutmeg. Toss the currants with 2 teaspoons of the sifted mixture.

Cream the butter in the large bowl of an electric mixer on moderate speed for 2 minutes. Add the sugar in two additions, beating for 1 minute after each portion is added. Beat in the eggs, one at a time, blending well after each addition. Blend in the vanilla extract and pumpkin. Add half of the sifted ingredients on low speed, beating until the particles of flour are absorbed. Blend in the sour cream and maple syrup. Add the balance of the sifted ingredients and mix until the particles of flour are absorbed. Stir in the currants.

Pour and scrape the batter into the prepared pan. Bake the cake for 1 hour, or until plump and a wooden pick inserted into the loaf emerges clean and dry.

Cool the cake in the pan on a rack for 4 to 5 minutes, invert onto another cooling rack and turn rightside up. Cool completely.

Store in an airtight container.

Rum Pound Cake

◆ *1 cake, serving 16* ◆

*T*ake this handsome cake to a pot luck supper. Summer's soft fruit—peaches, strawberries, plums—turned into a compote, would be an elegant accompaniment to the cake.

2 1/2 cups unsifted all-purpose
   flour
1/3 cup unsifted cake flour
1/2 teaspoon baking soda
3/4 teaspoon salt
3/4 teaspoon freshly grated nutmeg
1/2 pound (2 sticks) unsalted
   butter, softened

2 3/4 cups superfine sugar
6 extra-large eggs
2 teaspoons vanilla extract
1 1/2 tablespoons light rum
1 cup sour cream

FOR THE SUGAR AND RUM GLAZE:
3 tablespoons light rum
3 tablespoons granulated sugar

1 1/2 tablespoons water

Preheat the oven to 325 degrees. Butter and flour a 10-inch tube pan.

Sift together four times the all-purpose flour, cake flour, baking soda, salt and nutmeg.

Cream the butter in the large bowl of an electric mixer on moderate speed for 3 minutes. Add the sugar in four additions, beating for 2 minutes after each portion is added. Beat in the eggs, one at a time, blending well after each addition. Scrape down the sides of the mixing bowl often to keep the batter even-textured. Blend in the vanilla extract and rum. On low speed, alternately add the sifted ingredients in three additions with the sour cream in two additions, beginning and ending with the sifted mixture.

Pour and scrape the batter into the pan. Bake the cake for 1 hour and 20 minutes to 1 hour and 25 minutes, until nicely risen and golden, and a wooden pick inserted into the cake emerges clean and dry.

Cool the cake in the pan on a rack for 5 minutes, invert onto another cooling rack and turn rightside up.

For the glaze, combine the rum, sugar and water in a saucepan. Cover, place over low heat and cook until the grains of sugar have dissolved; uncover, raise the heat to high and bring to a boil. Spoon the hot glaze on top of the warm cake. Cool completely.

Store in an airtight container.

Coconut Keeping Cake

◆ *1 cake, serving 16* ◆

*W*hat preserves a pound cake in your memory? Its golden crust and hefty slice? Its aroma while baking? Or its close, moist crumb? I've refined this recipe over and over again to achieve just those things. This batter bakes into a tall, good-looking cake. It's one of the cakes my friends request during the Christmas season and superb to have on hand for serving with midmorning coffee or afternoon tea. For dessert, offer ambrosia or good vanilla ice cream with the cake.

3 3/4 cups sifted all-purpose flour
1/3 cup unsifted cake flour
1/8 teaspoon baking powder
1/2 teaspoon salt
1 teaspoon freshly grated nutmeg
3/4 pound (3 sticks) unsalted
   butter, softened
8 tablespoons (1 stick) margarine,
   softened
2 3/4 cups superfine sugar

3/4 cup light brown sugar
8 extra-large eggs
4 extra-large egg yolks
2 teaspoons vanilla extract
1 tablespoon heavy cream
1 1/3 cups sweetened flaked
   coconut
1 cup finely chopped
   macadamia nuts

Preheat the oven to 350 degrees. Butter and flour a 10-inch tube pan.

Resift the all-purpose flour with the cake flour, baking powder, salt and nutmeg.

Cream the butter and margarine in the large bowl of an electric mixer on moderately high speed for 5 minutes. Add the superfine sugar in two additions, beating for 2 minutes after each portion is added. Add the light brown sugar and beat for 2 minutes. Beat in the eggs, one at a time, blending well after each addition. Beat in the egg yolks, one at a time. Blend in the vanilla extract. On low speed, add the sifted ingredients in three additions, mixing until the particles of flour are absorbed. Blend in the heavy cream. Stir in the coconut and macadamia nuts.

Pour and scrape the batter into the prepared pan. Bake the cake for 1 hour and 40 minutes, or until a wooden pick inserted into the cake emerges clean and dry. The baked cake will pull away slightly from the sides of the baking pan.

Cool the cake in the pan on a rack for 5 minutes, invert onto another cooling rack and turn rightside up. Cool completely.

Store in an airtight container.

Three Nut Keeping Cake

◆ *1 cake, serving 16* ◆

*T*his cake is generously fortified with lots of eggs, butter and three different kinds of nuts. Autumn fruit desserts, such as glistening poached pears or stewed dried fruit are good to serve alongside thin slices of this pound cake. In the summer, serve with peaches, plums or nectarines macerated in a little light rum or white grape juice.

3 cups sifted cake flour
3/4 cup sifted all-purpose flour
3 tablespoons cornstarch
1/2 teaspoon baking powder
1 teaspoon salt
2 teaspoons ground cinnamon
1 teaspoon freshly grated nutmeg
1/4 teaspoon ground allspice
1 cup chopped walnuts
1 cup chopped pecans

1/2 cup chopped macadamia nuts
3/4 pound (3 sticks) unsalted
  butter, softened
8 tablespoons (1 stick) margarine,
  softened
2 1/2 cups superfine sugar
10 extra-large eggs
2 extra-large egg yolks
2 teaspoons vanilla extract

Preheat the oven to 325 degrees. Butter and flour a 10-inch tube pan.

Resift the cake flour with the all-purpose flour, cornstarch, baking powder, salt, cinnamon, nutmeg and allspice. Toss the walnuts, pecans and macadamia nuts with 2 tablespoons of the sifted mixture.

Cream the butter and margarine in the large bowl of an electric mixer on moderately high speed for 3 to 4 minutes. Add the sugar in three additions, beating for 1 to 2 minutes after each portion is added. Beat in the eggs, one at a time, blending well after each addition. Beat in the egg yolks. Blend in the vanilla extract. On low speed, alternately add the sifted ingredients in three additions, mixing just until the particles of flour are absorbed. Stir in the nuts.

Pour and scrape the batter into the prepared pan. Bake the cake for 1 hour and 15 minutes to 1 hour and 20 minutes, or until golden on top and a wooden pick inserted into the cake emerges clean and dry. The baked cake will pull away slightly from the sides of the pan.

Cool the cake in the pan on a rack for 5 to 7 minutes, invert onto another cooling rack and turn rightside up. Cool completely.

Store in an airtight container.

Toasted Pecan and
Chocolate Butter Cake

◆ *1 cake, serving 10* ◆

*T*opped with a generous sprinkling of confectioners' sugar, this genial cake is a delicious combination of pecans and miniature chocolate chips trapped in a moist and buttery batter. I've always baked this cake in a deeply swirled and fluted tube pan 9 inches in diameter; in it, the cake stands tall.

2 2/3 cups sifted all-purpose flour
1/3 cup plus 1 tablespoon unsifted
  cake flour
1 1/2 teaspoons baking powder
1/2 teaspoon salt
1 12-ounce bag miniature
  semisweet chocolate chips
3/4 cup chopped toasted pecans

1/2 pound (2 sticks) unsalted
  butter, softened
1 3/4 cups granulated sugar
1/3 cup light brown sugar
2 teaspoons vanilla extract
4 extra-large eggs
1 cup half-and-half

Preheat the oven to 350 degrees. Butter and flour a deep, fluted 9-inch tube pan.

Resift the all-purpose flour with the cake flour, baking powder and salt. Sift the mixture once again. Toss the chocolate chips and pecans with 1 tablespoon of the sifted mixture.

Cream the butter in the large bowl of an electric mixer on moderate speed for 5 minutes. Add the granulated sugar in two additions, beating for 2 minutes after each portion is added. Add the light brown sugar and continue beating on moderately high speed for 2 minutes longer. Blend in the vanilla extract. Beat in the eggs, one at a time, blending well after each addition. On low speed, alternately add the sifted ingredients in three additions with the half-and-half in two additions, beginning and ending with the sifted mixture. Stir in the chocolate chips and nuts.

Pour and scrape the batter into the prepared pan. Bake the cake for 1 hour and 5 minutes, or until a wooden pick inserted into the cake emerges without any clinging cake particles. (You'll run into a few chocolate chips, and the pick will withdraw moistened with chocolate, although the cake will be fully baked.) The baked cake will pull away slightly from the sides of the pan. (Quickly and carefully place a sheet of aluminum foil over the top of the cake during the last 20 to 25 minutes of baking time, if it appears to be browning too fast.)

Cool the cake in the pan on a rack for 4 to 5 minutes and invert onto another cooling rack. Cool completely.

Store in an airtight container.

Luxurious Vanilla Pound Cake

◆ *1 cake, serving 16* ◆

I have this lovely, old-time recipe for pound cake from my friend Mimi Davidson, who loves to serve it with berries and whipped cream. The recipe came to her many, many years ago in somewhat different form—the amounts of some ingredients were approximate, as was the baking time and temperature. We worked out the formula that you see here, adding the seed scrapings of a vanilla bean to boost the flavor of the cake and replacing part of the all-purpose flour with cake flour. We love its old-fashioned flavor and its fine keeping qualities.

3 3/4 cups sifted all-purpose flour
1/4 cup unsifted cake flour
2 1/2 teaspoons baking powder
1 teaspoon salt
1/2 pound (2 sticks) unsalted butter, softened

2 cups superfine sugar
6 extra-large eggs
1 tablespoon vanilla extract
Seed scrapings from a small vanilla bean
1 cup milk

Preheat the oven to 350 degrees. Butter and flour a 10-inch tube pan.

Resift the all-purpose flour and cake flour with the baking powder and salt.

Cream the butter in the large bowl of an electric mixer on moderately high speed for 5 minutes. Add the sugar in three additions, beating for 2 minutes after each portion is added. Beat in the eggs, one at a time, blending well after each addition. Blend in the vanilla extract and vanilla bean scrapings. On low speed, alternately add the sifted ingredients in three additions with the milk in two additions, beginning and ending with the sifted mixture.

Pour and scrape the batter into the prepared pan. Bake the cake for 1 hour and 15 minutes, or until golden on top and a wooden pick inserted into the cake emerges clean and dry. The baked cake will pull away slightly from the sides of the pan.

Cool the cake in the pan on a rack for 5 to 7 minutes, invert onto another cooling rack, and turn rightside up. Cool completely.

Store in an airtight container.

Classic Sour Cream Pound Cake

◆ *1 cake, serving 16* ◆

*S*our cream in the cake batter makes this pound cake moist and rich. It's delicious served with ice cream and a spoonful of hot fudge sauce; stewed prunes or a mixture of poached apricots and peaches; or sliced strawberries and heavy cream, softly whipped and flavored with vanilla extract.

*2 1/2 cups unsifted all-purpose
    flour
1/2 cup unsifted cake flour
1/2 teaspoon baking powder
1/4 teaspoon baking soda
1/2 teaspoon salt
1/2 teaspoon freshly grated nutmeg
1/2 pound (2 sticks) unsalted
    butter, softened*

*1/2 cup solid shortening
3 cups less 2 tablespoons superfine
    sugar
5 extra-large eggs
2 teaspoons vanilla extract
1 cup sour cream*

Preheat the oven to 325 degrees. Butter and flour a 10-inch tube pan.

Sift together twice the all-purpose flour, cake flour, baking powder, baking soda, salt and nutmeg.

Cream the butter and shortening in the large bowl of an electric mixer on moderately high speed for 4 minutes. Add the sugar in four additions, beating for 2 minutes after each portion is added. Beat the butter-sugar mixture on high speed for 2 minutes. Beat in the eggs, one at a time, blending well after each addition. Blend in the vanilla extract. On low speed, alternately add the sifted ingredients in three additions with the sour cream in two additions, beginning and ending with the sifted mixture.

Pour and scrape the batter into the prepared pan. Bake the cake for 1 hour 25 minutes to 1 hour and 30 minutes, or until golden on top and a wooden pick inserted into the cake emerges clean and dry. The baked cake will pull away slightly from the sides of the pan.

Cool the cake in the pan on a rack for 5 minutes, invert onto another cooling rack and turn rightside up. Cool completely.

Store in an airtight container.

VARIATIONS

For *Classic Sour Cream Pound Cake with Nuts*, toss 1 cup chopped, lightly toasted walnuts or pecans with 1 tablespoon of the sifted mixture. Stir the nuts into the batter after the flour and sour cream have been added.

For *Classic Sour Cream Pound Cake with Miniature Chocolate Chips*, toss 1 1/2 cups miniature semisweet chocolate chips with 1 tablespoon of the sifted mixture. Stir the chips into the batter after the flour and sour cream have been added.

For *Classic Sour Cream Pound Cake with Miniature Chocolate Chips and Nuts*, toss 1 1/4 cups miniature semisweet chocolate chips and 3/4 cups chopped, lightly toasted walnuts or pecans with 1 tablespoon of the sifted mixture. Stir the chips and nuts into the batter after the flour and sour cream have been added.

For *Classic Lemon Sour Cream Pound Cake*, substitute lemon extract for the vanilla extract. Add 1 tablespoon grated lemon peel to the batter along with the lemon extract. Bake as directed. About 10 minutes after the cake has been removed from the pan, spoon a mixture of 3 tablespoons lemon juice and 3 tablespoons granulated sugar over the top of the cake.

· 7 ·

Sweet and Savory
Yeast Breads and Rolls

A bundle of rolls or a handsome loaf of bread, with a handmade look and yeasty aroma, is a delight to receive. A breakfast bread, such as the *Walnut Coffeecake Loaf* (page 108), *Honey Buns* (page 112) or *Jumbo Cinnamon and Pecan Rolls* (page 110) is a tempting gift to give a weekend host or hostess. The *Whole Wheat Bread with Herbs, Nuts and Seeds* (page 98), or *Green Pepper and Pimiento-Flecked Cheese Bread* (page 100) is a superb bread to bring to a pot luck dinner and is marvelous paired with robust soups, stews or ragouts.

For a festive appearance, most any bread dough can be braided or twisted and baked directly on cookie sheets rather than in conventional loaf pans. The dough for rolls, too, takes well to fashioning into fancy shapes, such as fantans, coils or rosebuds. Rolls are baked in standard muffin tins, but you can certainly vary the size of the tin—from the tiny gem-size pan to the giant Texas muffin or bun-size pan. And some doughs, although designed to be made into loaves, bake up nicely as rolls—especially the *Bran and Oatmeal*

Bread (page 96) and *Whole Wheat Bread with Herbs, Nuts and Seeds* (page 98). Generally, you bake rolls formed in muffin tins (measuring 2 3/4 inches in diameter and 1 3/4 inches deep) in a 400-degree oven for about 13 to 15 minutes.

For gift-giving, cool the just-baked bread, then bag or wrap the rolls to preserve freshness. When presenting the bread as a gift, always furnish a small instructional note about reheating: Most breads can be reheated in a 350-degree oven, loosely covered in aluminum foil, for about 15 minutes. Rolls take a little less time, about 10 minutes.

◆–◆–◆

Cinnamon Swirl Bread

◆ 2 loaves, each serving 6 to 8 ◆

The spiral of cinnamon-sugar and raisins that winds through each loaf sweetens and spices a fine white yeast dough. Sliced and toasted, it makes a gratifying breakfast bread. These loaves freeze particularly well.

FOR THE DOUGH:

3 1/2 teaspoons active dry yeast
1/4 cup plus 1 teaspoon granulated
    sugar
1/3 cup warm (110 to 115
    degrees) water
1 cup milk
1/4 cup evaporated milk
1/4 cup water

7 tablespoons unsalted butter
2 extra-large eggs
1 teaspoon vanilla extract
2 cups unsifted bread flour
1 1/2 teaspoons salt
3 3/4 cups unsifted all-purpose
    flour

FOR THE SUGAR AND SPICE FILLING:

5 tablespoons unsalted butter,
    melted and cooled
2/3 cup granulated sugar blended
    with 2 tablespoons light brown
    sugar, 1 tablespoon ground
    cinnamon and 1/2 teaspoon
    freshly grated nutmeg

2/3 cup dark raisins

TO FINISH THE LOAVES:

2 tablespoons unsalted butter,
    melted

Mix the yeast, 1 teaspoon of the sugar and warm water in a bowl and set aside for 4 to 5 minutes for the yeast to dissolve and swell.

Place the milk, evaporated milk, 1/4 cup water, remaining 1/4 cup sugar and butter in a saucepan and scald. Cool the milk mixture to lukewarm, then beat in the eggs and vanilla extract. Blend in the yeast mixture.

Mix the bread flour, salt and 2 cups all-purpose flour in a large bowl. Pour the yeast-milk mixture over the dry ingredients. Stir well. Add the remaining 1 3/4 cups of all-purpose flour, a little at a time, to form a dough that is no longer sticky to the touch (but still reasonably soft), adding additional flour if necessary. Knead the dough on a lightly floured work surface for 8 to 9 minutes, or until resilient.

Place the dough in a greased bowl. Cover and let rise until doubled in bulk, about 1 hour and 10 minutes to 1 hour and 20 minutes.

Butter and flour two 9-by-5-by-3-inch loaf pans.

Punch down the dough and divide into two parts. Roll each part into a rectangle, brush with half of the melted butter, sprinkle with half of the sugar and spice blend, and scatter over half of the raisins. Roll up each rectangle and fit into a prepared loaf pan. Cover and let rise until doubled in bulk, about 1 hour and 10 minutes.

Preheat the oven to 375 degrees.

Paint the top of the bread with the melted butter, using a soft pastry brush. Bake the bread for 40 minutes, or until golden on top and each loaf sounds hollow when tapped with your knuckles.

Cool the breads in the pans on a rack for 5 minutes. Remove the loaves from the pans and place on cooling racks. Cool completely.

Wrap each loaf and store in a container.

Bran and Oatmeal Bread

◆ *2 loaves, each serving 4 to 6* ◆

*G*ood old-fashioned oats and a generous sprinkling of bran give this bread its character. Toast it for breakfast or cut it into thick slices and serve with hearty soups and stews.

2 3/4 teaspoons active dry yeast	2 tablespoons vegetable oil
1/4 cup plus 1 teaspoon granulated sugar	1 1/4 cups milk, scalded
1/4 cup warm (110 to 115 degrees) water	2 extra-large eggs
	3 cups unsifted bread flour
1 1/4 cups "old-fashioned" rolled oats	1/3 cup bran (not bran cereal)
	1 1/2 teaspoons salt
2 tablespoons unsalted butter	1/2 teaspoon ground allspice
	1 cup unsifted all-purpose flour

Mix the yeast, 1 teaspoon of the sugar and warm water in a bowl and set aside for 4 to 5 minutes for the yeast to dissolve and swell.

Place the oats, butter, oil and remaining 1/4 cup sugar in a bowl. Stir in the milk and let stand for 10 minutes. Stir in the eggs and yeast mixture.

Mix the bread flour, bran, salt and allspice in a large bowl. Stir in the oat mixture. Mix in the all-purpose flour, a little at a time, to form a dough that is no longer sticky to the touch, adding more flour if necessary. Knead the dough on a lightly floured work surface for 10 minutes. The dough will be firm and offer some resistance.

Place the dough in a greased bowl. Cover and let rise until doubled in bulk, about 1 hour and 30 minutes.

Butter and flour two 8-by-4-by-3-inch loaf pans.

Punch down the dough and divide into two parts. Form each part into a loaf and place in a prepared pan. Cover and let rise until doubled in bulk, about 1 hour.

Preheat the oven to 350 degrees.

Bake the bread for 40 minutes, or until golden on top and each loaf sounds hollow when tapped with your knuckles.

Cool the breads in the pans on a rack for 5 minutes. Remove the loaves from the pans and place on cooling racks. Cool completely.

Wrap each loaf and store in a container.

Whole Wheat Bread
with Herbs, Nuts and Seeds

◆ *1 loaf, serving 6 to 8* ◆

*T*his fragrant bread is so very good with soups, or anything from the casserole, such as a stew or ragout. Now and then, I bake the dough in fancy fluted loaf pans, a large brioche mold, or in a large free-form braid, twisted into a circle on a cookie sheet; the latter makes a particularly festive gift.

2 1/2 teaspoons active dry yeast
3/4 teaspoon granulated sugar
1/3 cup warm (110 to 115
*   degrees) water*
1 cup milk
3 tablespoons vegetable oil
2 tablespoons unsalted butter
1 extra-large egg
1 extra-large egg yolk
1/4 cup chopped parsley
2 tablespoons chopped savory
*   leaves*

2 tablespoons chopped thyme leaves
1 teaspoon dried minced onions
1 1/2 cups unsifted whole wheat
*   flour*
1 1/2 teaspoons salt
1/2 cup chopped walnuts
1/4 cup roasted sunflower seeds
2 1/2 to 2 3/4 cups unsifted
*   all-purpose flour*

Mix the yeast, sugar and warm water in a bowl and set aside for 4 to 5 minutes for the yeast to dissolve and swell.

Place the milk, oil and butter in a saucepan and scald. Cool to lukewarm. Blend in the egg, egg yolk, parsley, savory, thyme, minced onions and yeast mixture.

Mix the whole wheat flour, salt, walnuts, sunflower seeds and 1 cup all-purpose flour in a large bowl. Pour the yeast-egg mixture over the dry ingredients. Stir well. Add 1 1/2 cups of all-purpose flour, a little at a time, to form a dough that is no longer sticky to the touch, adding the remaining 1/4 cup flour if necessary. Knead the dough on a lightly floured work surface for 10 minutes, or until bouncy.

Place the dough in a greased bowl. Cover and let rise until doubled in bulk, about 1 hour and 20 minutes.

Butter and flour a 9-by-5-by-3-inch loaf pan.

Punch down the dough, form into a loaf and place in the prepared pan. Cover and let rise until doubled in bulk, about 1 hour and 15 minutes to 1 hour and 30 minutes.

Preheat the oven to 350 degrees.

Bake the bread for 35 to 40 minutes, or until the loaf sounds hollow when tapped with your knuckles.

Cool the bread in the pan on a rack for 5 minutes. Remove the loaf from the pan and place on a cooling rack. Cool completely.

Wrap the loaf and store in a container.

Green Pepper and
Pimiento-Flecked Cheese Bread

◆ *1 loaf, serving 6 to 8* ◆

*A*s this bread bakes, it fills the kitchen with a savory scent. When freshly baked, the loaf needs nothing more than sweet butter to accompany it. Sliced and toasted, it is good to have on hand for turkey or chicken sandwiches.

2 1/2 teaspoons active dry yeast
3/4 teaspoon granulated sugar
1/4 cup warm (110 to 115
  degrees) water
2/3 cup milk
3 tablespoons water
4 tablespoons solid shortening
1 extra-large egg
1 tablespoon Dijon mustard
1 cup unsifted bread flour
1 teaspoon salt

1/4 teaspoon cayenne pepper
2 3/4 cups unsifted all-purpose
  flour
3/4 cup packed shredded swiss
  cheese, such as Gruyère (use the
  large holes of a hand grater)
3 tablespoons minced canned
  pimientos
3 tablespoons minced green bell
  pepper

Mix the yeast, sugar and warm water in a bowl and set aside for 4 to 5 minutes for the yeast to dissolve and swell.

Place the milk, water and shortening in a saucepan and scald. Cool to lukewarm. Blend in the egg, mustard and yeast mixture.

Mix the bread flour, salt, cayenne pepper and 1 1/2 cups all-purpose flour in a large mixing bowl. Pour the yeast-milk mixture over the dry ingredients.

Add the cheese, pimientos and bell pepper. Stir well. Add the remaining 1 1/4 cups all-purpose flour, a little at a time, to form a dough that is no longer sticky to the touch. Knead the dough on a lightly floured work surface for 8 to 10 minutes, or until supple and resilient.

Place the dough in a greased bowl. Cover and let rise until doubled in bulk, about 1 hour and 25 minutes.

Butter and flour a 9-by-5-by-3-inch loaf pan.

Punch down the dough, form into a loaf and place in the prepared pan. Cover and let rise until doubled in bulk, about 1 hour.

Preheat the oven to 375 degrees.

Bake the bread for 35 minutes, or until golden on top and the loaf sounds hollow when tapped with your knuckles.

Cool the bread in the pans on a rack for 4 to 5 minutes. Remove the loaf from the pan and place on a cooling rack. Cool completely.

Wrap the loaf and store in a container.

Tomato Rolls

◆ *about 2 dozen 2 3/4-inch rolls* ◆

*T*he dough for these rolls is tinted with tomato juice and tomato paste, and seasoned lightly with oregano and thyme. The rolls freeze very well, and are pleasing served with winter stews, roasted chicken or turkey and summery composed salads.

2 1/2 teaspoons active dry yeast
1 teaspoon granulated sugar
1/4 cup warm (110 to 115 degrees) water
3/4 cup tomato juice blended with 2 teaspoons tomato paste
1/3 cup water
5 tablespoons solid shortening

3 tablespoons butter
1 teaspoon dried oregano leaves
1 teaspoon dried thyme leaves
2 extra-large eggs
1 cup unsifted bread flour
1 teaspoon salt
3 1/2 cups unsifted all-purpose flour

Mix the yeast, sugar and warm water in a bowl and set aside for 4 to 5 minutes for the yeast to dissolve and swell.

Place the tomato juice–tomato paste blend, water, shortening and butter in a saucepan and scald. Cool slightly. Blend in the oregano and thyme. Blend in the eggs and yeast mixture.

Mix the bread flour, salt and 1 1/2 cups all-purpose flour in a large bowl. Pour the yeast–tomato juice mixture over the dry ingredients. Mix well. Add the remaining 2 cups all-purpose flour, a little at a time, to form a dough that is no longer sticky to the touch. Knead the dough on a lightly floured work surface for 10 minutes, or until bouncy.

Place the dough in a greased bowl. Cover and let rise until doubled in bulk, about 1 hour and 30 minutes.

Butter and flour 24 muffin cups measuring 2 3/4 inches in diameter and 1 3/8 inches deep.

Punch down the dough. Divide the dough into 36 pieces. Roll each piece into a fat sausage, twist and coil into a knot. Place a roll in each cup as it is formed. Cover and let rise until doubled in bulk, about 45 minutes to 1 hour.

Preheat the oven to 375 degrees.

Bake the rolls for 15 minutes, or until firm to the touch.

Cool the rolls in the pans on a rack for 3 to 4 minutes. Remove the rolls from the muffin tins and place on cooling racks.

Bag the rolls and store in a container.

Potato Rolls

♦ *about 2 dozen 2 3/4-inch rolls* ♦

*T*his dough is a delight to knead and form into rolls, for it is supple and bouncy. Using the water in which the potatoes have cooked for part of the liquid in the recipe produces this springy quality and, on baking, creates a fine-textured roll. For a change, the dough can be flavored with chopped fresh herbs.

2 3/4 teaspoons active dry yeast
1 1/2 teaspoons granulated sugar
1/4 cup warm (110 to 115 degrees) water
1/2 cup unseasoned mashed potatoes
3/4 cup potato-cooking water (see note below)
1/4 cup light cream

1 tablespoon honey
7 tablespoons unsalted butter
1 extra-large egg
4 1/2 cups unsifted all-purpose flour
1 1/2 teaspoons salt
1/4 teaspoon freshly ground black pepper

Mix the yeast, sugar and the warm water in a bowl and set aside for 4 to 5 minutes for the yeast to dissolve and swell.

Mix the mashed potatoes, potato-cooking water, cream, honey and butter in a saucepan and heat until hot. Remove from the heat and cool to lukewarm. Beat in the egg and yeast mixture.

Stir together 3 cups all-purpose flour, salt and pepper in a large mixing bowl. Stir in the potato-yeast mixture. Add enough of the remaining 1 1/2 cups all-purpose flour, a little at a time, to form a dough that is no longer sticky to the touch, adding extra sprinkles of flour as necessary. Knead the dough on a lightly floured work surface for 8 to 10 minutes, or until resilient.

Place the dough in a greased bowl. Cover and let rise until doubled in bulk, about 1 hour and 15 minutes to 1 hour and 25 minutes.

Butter and flour 30 muffin cups measuring 2 3/4 inches in diameter and 1 3/8 inches deep.

Punch down the dough. Divide the dough into 24 pieces and divide each piece into 2 sections; roll each section into a ball. Place 2 balls of dough in each muffin cup. Cover and let rise until doubled in bulk, about 1 hour.

Preheat the oven to 400 degrees.

Bake the rolls about 12 minutes, or until golden. Cool the rolls in the pans on a rack for 3 to 4 minutes. Remove the rolls from the muffin tins and place on cooling racks. Cool completely.

Bag the rolls and store in a container.

NOTE: The water in which the potatoes have been boiled creates a dough with a fine "crumb." Once the potatoes are cooked until very tender, remove them with a slotted spoon and mash well. Measure out 3/4 cup of the cooking water to use in the recipe.

Oatmeal Rolls

◆ *about 14 2 3/4-inch rolls* ◆

*T*hese rolls are reminiscent of oatmeal cookies, with molasses and brown sugar flavoring the dough. Serve them warm at breakfast with a slathering of honey butter or a bright-tasting jam.

2 1/2 teaspoons active dry yeast	4 tablespoons solid shortening
1 1/2 teaspoons granulated sugar	3/4 cup boiling water
1/3 cup warm (110 to 115 degrees) water	1/2 cup unsifted whole wheat flour
	1/4 cup unsifted bread flour
3/4 cup "old-fashioned" rolled oats	1 1/2 teaspoons salt
1 tablespoon light molasses	2 cups unsifted all-purpose flour
3 tablespoons light brown sugar	1/2 cup dark raisins

Mix the yeast, 1 1/2 teaspoons granulated sugar and warm water in a bowl and set aside for 4 to 5 minutes for the yeast to dissolve and swell.

Place the oats, molasses, 3 tablespoons light brown sugar and shortening in a bowl, add the boiling water and stir. Cool to lukewarm. Stir in the yeast mixture.

Mix the whole wheat flour, bread flour, salt and 1 cup all-purpose flour in a large bowl. Pour the oat-yeast mixture over the dry ingredients. Mix well. Add the remaining cup of all-purpose flour, a little at a time, to form a dough that is no longer sticky to the touch, adding more flour if necessary. Knead the dough on a lightly floured work surface for 8 to 10 minutes, or until supple.

Place the dough in a greased bowl. Cover and let rise until doubled in bulk, about 1 hour to 1 hour and 20 minutes.

Butter and flour 14 muffin cups measuring 2 3/4 inches in diameter and 1 3/8 inches deep.

Punch down the dough and knead in the raisins; divide the dough into 14 equal pieces. Cut each piece in half and roll into balls. Place 2 balls of dough in each cup. Cover and let rise until doubled in bulk, about 1 hour.

Preheat the oven to 375 degrees.

Bake the rolls for 16 to 18 minutes, or until golden on top.

Cool the rolls in the pans on a rack for 3 to 4 minutes. Remove the rolls from the muffin tins and place on cooling racks.

Bag the rolls and store in a container.

Walnut Coffeecake Loaf

◆ *1 loaf, serving 6 to 8* ◆

*S*wirls of a nut-flecked cream cheese and butter filling flavor this lightly sweetened yeast dough.

FOR THE DOUGH:

2 1/2 teaspoons active dry yeast
3 tablespoons plus 1 teaspoon granulated sugar
1/4 cup warm (110 to 115 degrees) water
1/2 cup milk
6 tablespoons (3/4 stick) unsalted butter, cut into chunks

1 extra-large egg
1 extra-large egg yolk
1/2 teaspoon vanilla extract
1/2 cup unsifted bread flour
1/2 teaspoon salt
2 3/4 cups unsifted all-purpose flour

FOR THE WALNUT FILLING:

1 3-ounce package cream cheese, softened
2 tablespoons unsalted butter, softened
1/4 cup granulated sugar blended with 1 teaspoon ground cinnamon

1 extra-large egg yolk
1/4 teaspoon vanilla extract
2/3 cup chopped walnuts

Mix the yeast, 1 teaspoon of the sugar and warm water in a bowl and set aside for 4 to 5 minutes for the yeast to dissolve and swell.

Place the milk, butter and remaining 3 tablespoons sugar in a saucepan and scald. Cool to lukewarm. Blend in the egg, egg yolk and vanilla extract.

Mix the bread flour, salt and 3/4 cup all-purpose flour in a large mixing bowl. Pour the yeast-milk mixture over the dry ingredients. Stir well. Add the remaining 2 cups of all-purpose flour, a little at a time, to form a dough that is no longer sticky to the touch. Knead the dough on a lightly floured work surface for 8 to 10 minutes, or until supple and resilient.

Place the dough in a greased bowl. Cover and let rise until doubled in bulk, about 1 hour and 30 minutes to 1 hour and 50 minutes.

For the filling, beat together the cream cheese, butter and cinnamon-sugar blend in a small mixing bowl. Beat in the egg yolk and vanilla extract. Set aside.

Butter and flour a 10-by-5-by-3-inch loaf pan.

Punch down the dough and roll into a 12-inch square. Spread the filling over the surface of the dough and sprinkle with the walnuts. Roll up the dough as for a jellyroll and cut into 8 slices. Place the slices in the pan, over-lapping them slightly. Cover and let rise until doubled in bulk, about 1 hour and 30 minutes to 2 hours.

Preheat the oven to 350 degrees.

Bake the bread for 40 minutes, or until golden on top and the loaf sounds hollow when tapped with your knuckles.

Cool the loaf in the pan on a rack for 5 minutes. Remove the loaf from the pan and place on a cooling rack. Cool completely.

Wrap the loaf and store in a container.

VARIATION

For *Walnut Coffeecake Loaf with Currants or Raisins*, sprinkle 1/3 cup moist, dried currants or raisins with the walnuts over the cream cheese filling.

Jumbo Cinnamon and Pecan Rolls

◆ *1/2 dozen 4-inch rolls* ◆

These fat and yeasty rolls, stuffed with raisins and pecans, would make a fine weekend breakfast treat.

FOR THE YEAST DOUGH:

2 1/2 teaspoons active dry yeast
1/4 cup plus 1 teaspoon granulated
    sugar
1/4 cup warm (110 to 115
    degrees) water
1/2 cup milk
3 tablespoons water

4 tablespoons (1/2 stick) unsalted
    butter
4 tablespoons solid shortening
1 extra-large egg
3 cups unsifted all-purpose flour
1 teaspoon salt

FOR THE CINNAMON AND PECAN FILLING:

4 tablespoons unsalted butter,
    softened
1/3 cup granulated sugar blended
    with 1 tablespoon ground
    cinnamon

1/2 cup chopped pecans
1/3 cup dark raisins

Mix the yeast, 1 teaspoon of the sugar and warm water in a small bowl and set aside for 4 to 5 minutes for the yeast to dissolve and swell.

Place the milk, 3 tablespoons water, remaining 1/4 cup sugar, 4 tablespoons butter and shortening in a saucepan and heat until the fat melts. Remove from the heat and cool to lukewarm. Beat in the egg and the yeast mixture.

Mix 2 cups all-purpose flour and the salt in a large mixing bowl. Pour the yeast-milk mixture over the dry ingredients and stir to form a dough. Add the remaining cup of all-purpose flour, a little at a time, to form a dough that is no longer sticky to the touch, adding extra flour if necessary. Knead the dough on a lightly floured work surface for 8 to 10 minutes, or until springy and resilient.

Place the dough in a greased bowl. Cover and let rise until doubled in bulk, about 1 hour and 10 minutes to 1 hour and 20 minutes.

Butter and flour 6 jumbo muffin cups measuring a scant 4 inches in diameter and 1 3/4 inches deep.

Punch down the dough. Roll the dough into a 12-inch square on a lightly floured work surface. Spread the butter on the dough. Sprinkle with the cinnamon-sugar blend, pecans and raisins. Roll up the dough, as for a jellyroll. Cut the log of dough into 6 slices. Place each slice in a muffin cup. Cover and let rise until doubled in bulk, about 1 hour and 15 minutes to 1 hour and 30 minutes.

Preheat the oven to 350 degrees.

Bake the rolls for 35 minutes, or until golden brown.

Cool the rolls in the pan on a rack for 3 to 4 minutes. Remove the rolls from the pan and place on a cooling rack. Cool completely.

Bag the rolls and store in a container.

Honey Buns

◆ *1 1/2 dozen 3 1/2- to 4-inch buns* ◆

*S*oftly sweet buns, fragrant with cinnamon and sweetened with honey, make a splendid breakfast bread to serve on lazy Sunday mornings. The rolls are placed in a baking pan, and as they rise, merge into a puffy square reminiscent of a coffee cake. Serve the rolls in the entire cake, and encourage each guest to break apart his or her own helping.

FOR THE DOUGH:

3 teaspoons active dry yeast
1 3/4 teaspoons granulated sugar
1/3 cup warm (110 to 115
   degrees) water
1 1/4 cups milk
5 tablespoons unsalted butter, cut
   into chunks
3 tablespoons solid shortening

1/3 cup honey
1 extra-large egg
1 extra-large egg yolk
1 1/2 cups unsifted bread flour
3/4 teaspoon salt
2 tablespoons ground cinnamon
3 1/2 cups unsifted all-purpose
   flour

FOR THE FILLING:

10 tablespoons (1 1/4 sticks)
   unsalted butter, softened
2 tablespoons ground cinnamon
1/3 cup honey

3 tablespoons light brown sugar
1/3 cup granulated sugar
1/4 teaspoon vanilla extract
1 cup moist dried currants

For the dough, mix the yeast, sugar and warm water in a bowl and set aside for 4 to 5 minutes for the yeast to dissolve and swell.

Place the milk, butter, shortening and honey in a saucepan and scald. Cool to lukewarm. Beat in the egg, egg yolk and yeast mixture.

Mix the bread flour, salt, cinnamon and 2 cups of the all-purpose flour in a large mixing bowl. Pour the milk-yeast mixture over the dry ingredients. Mix well. Add the remaining 1 1/2 cups all-purpose flour, a little at a time, to form a dough that is no longer sticky to the touch, adding more flour if necessary. Knead the dough on a lightly floured work surface for 8 minutes, or until supple.

Place the dough in a greased bowl. Cover and let rise until doubled in bulk, about 1 hour and 45 minutes.

For the filling, cream the butter and cinnamon in a mixing bowl. Beat in the honey, sugars and vanilla extract.

Butter and flour two 9-inch square baking pans.

Punch down the dough. Roll it into a sheet roughly measuring 17 by 22 inches. Spread the filling over the surface of the dough and sprinkle with the currants. Roll up the dough as for a jellyroll and cut into 18 slices. Place 9 slices in each of the prepared pans. Cover and let rise until doubled in bulk, about 1 hour and 30 minutes.

Preheat the oven to 375 degrees.

Bake the buns for 30 to 35 minutes, or until golden and set.

Cool the buns in the pans on a rack for 3 to 4 minutes. Invert each square of buns onto a cooling rack, then invert again to cool rightside up. Cool completely.

Bag each "cake" of buns and store in a container.

Index